"*Black Punk Now* delivers a unique literary experience, full of sociopolitical insights, arresting visuals, and limitless imagination. By turns sharp, rousing, delightful, and electric, this is an anthology to savor."

—Dawnie Walton, author of *The Final Revival of Opal & Nev*

"In *Black Punk Now* Spooner and Terry have given voice, sound, fury, and shape to all things Black and BIPOC punk. Equal parts how-to guide, field manual, and encyclopedic anthology comprising essays, short stories, interviews, memories, and graphic novel panels. From the historical origins of those who paved the way, to those individuals and groups carrying the torch and keeping the flame alive. To have such an emotive, resonant, and necessary resource is as revolutionary as those of us melanated 'outsiders' who defy convention, stereotype, hyphenate, or box with our very being."

—Justin Warfield, musician and hip hop MC, She Wants Revenge

"A testament to the often challenging experience of being an outsider, and the joy of finding a sense of belonging. These are the stories I wish I heard when I was growing up."

—Nabil Ayers, author of *My Life in the Sunshine*

"When I got the book I jumped into it immediately. *Black Punk Now* solidifies the idea that even though alternative Black culture is multifaceted and unique, so many of us have the same story, just told different ways. I will always love reading Black stories but alternative Black stories hit home differently in a beautiful way. I really loved it, it was a fun read!"

—Braxton Marcellous, musician for ZULU, Wise, and Shred Bundy

"I'm slightly angry for being pushed to cry in public many times while reading this book, and for the amount of conversations holding *Black Punk Now* has sparked. I've had as many conversations with strangers outside of this book as I did with those inside of it. Thank you for this work which enables me to see myself, to see my brother. I grew up on music and comics and with a deep feeling of isolation. There is great beauty in the outskirts. The fringe. The edge. And there's loneliness and questioning of yourself and the world—of how you look, of how you feel, and of who you can confide in. Thank you for the hours that I spent inside of this collective work, feeling less alone. Thanks for also making this a relentless read in a soft way."   —Jean Grae, aka The Monarchy

"I really dig Black Punk Now it surprises illuminates informs and relates. You can dive in anywhere in the book and there you are right inside the fierce wit, energy, and force of those countering 'culture' the looks sounds and feels from the richest places, the nutrient-dense sediment where the money doesn't reside. Where you/they/we only gaf about not gaf. Jumping the future."

—Ishmael Butler, musician for Digable Planets and Shabazz Palaces

"Even now, as I'm finally exhaling—finally stretching, breathing, blinking—after the chaotic voyage James and Chris and all the lyrical alchemists in between took me on, I'm smacked in the mouth, again, by the title. Is *Black Punk Now* an acknowledgment of time, a chronicle of sorts of the present, or is it a shout? A motherfuckin' demand? One of the many beauties of this collection is that its title mirrors what it means to be Black and punk. Which means it means whatever you want it to be, as long as it's free."   —Damon Young, author of
What Doesn't Kill You Makes
You Blacker: A Memoir in Essays

BLACK
PUNK
NOW

BLACK PUNK NOW

FICTION, NONFICTION, AND COMICS

EDITED BY
JAMES SPOONER
CHRIS L. TERRY

SOFT SKULL
NEW YORK

First Soft Skull edition: 2023

Library of Congress Cataloging-in-Publication Data
Names: Terry, Chris L., editor. | Spooner, James, editor.
Title: Black punk now : fiction, nonfiction, and comics / edited by James
    Spooner, Chris L. Terry.
Description: First Soft Skull edition. | New York : Soft Skull, 2023.
Identifiers: LCCN 2023018942 | ISBN 9781593767457 (trade paperback) | ISBN
    9781593767464 (ebook)
Subjects: LCSH: Punk rock music—United States—History and criticism. |
    African American punk rock musicians. | Punk culture—United States. |
    Music and race—United States. | Punk rock music—United States—Fiction. |
    African American punk rock musicians—Fiction.
Classification: LCC ML3534.3 .B523 2023 | DDC 781.66089/960973—dc23/
    eng/20230502
LC record available at https://lccn.loc.gov/2023018942

Cover design by www.houseofthought.io
Cover photograph © Ed Marshall Photography NYC
Illustrations by James Spooner
Book design by tracy danes and Laura Berry

Published by Soft Skull Press
New York, NY
www.softskull.com

Printed in the United States of America

10 9 8 7 6 5 4 3 2 1

CONTENTS

INTRO

GENERATIONS

Inheritance. Relationships. Grief.

IN THE PIT

Solidarity. Togetherness. Creativity.

FIND YOURSELF

Community. Identity. Mental Health.

LIBERATION

Imagination. Activism. Tech.

OUTRO

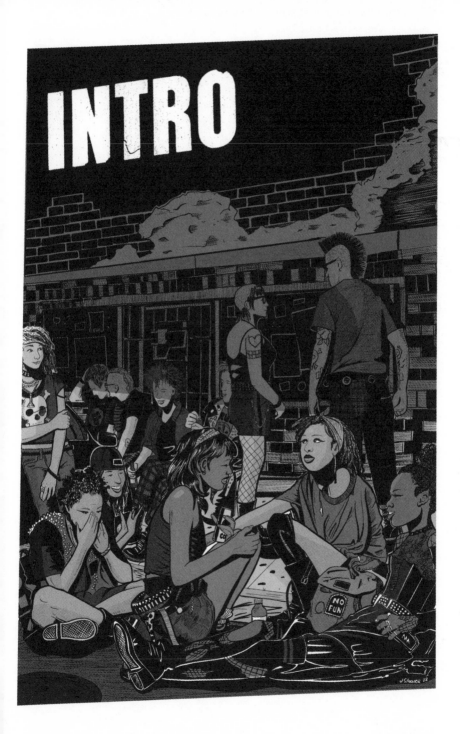

EDITORS' NOTES

After *Afro-Punk*

BOUGHT A COMPUTER ON CREDIT IN 2001. ONE OF THE FIRST THINGS I did, after sparking up my dial-up modem, was Google "Black Punk." There were exactly zero links. In all of the World Wide Web, I was alone. Living in New York City, I knew I wasn't the only one, but sitting there, in front of my Macintosh G3, it felt that way. I had to tell our story.

I lived in a newly gentrified building in Williamsburg, Brooklyn, but all the old tenants hadn't moved out as planned. There were rats pounding, screaming, suffocating in the walls. At times, I could relate to them more than to my roommates.

I was angry—punks usually are—about something. I had a documentary in mind. The film was meant to be a critique of the punk community, the people I'd come to think of as family. At this point, twenty-three years old with a decade in the scene, my love had soured and I began to resent all these white kids who "didn't see race."

I went on the hunt for people like me, who identified as Black and punk. I found a kid in Iowa, who was in six bands and essentially ran the Midwest scene. I found a collective of women in New York's outer boroughs who'd started a showcase to promote themselves as Black female solo artists. I found a Black hacker whose brother was in a Black Power hardcore band—with a bunch of white guys. Their stories were my story and mine was theirs. All told, I interviewed just short of ninety people and strung their stories together into a documentary, unknowingly giving us and so many others an identity—Afro-Punk.

Afro-Punk gave us a much-needed framework for conversation. In the spirit of DIY, I used the documentary as a springboard to build a Black community within the scene. It was working. For years in the mid '00s, Black alternative kids from all around the country would eagerly anticipate Afro-Punk events. I called them the Liberation Sessions, because what is more liberating than a mosh pit full of smiling Black faces? The bands were the fans and the fans were the bands. While we were in those rooms, no one thought about how white punks saw us. No one cared if they knew we existed. We defined ourselves. It was everything punk rock should be.

Screenings turned into concerts and concerts turned into a festival. *Afro-Punk* the film morphed into AFROPUNK™ the brand and, as mainstream interest grew, the dangling carrot of capitalism lured me in. I wanted it to grow. I wanted all the Black weirdos across America to feel what we were feeling in those rooms. But organic growth and corporate sponsorship don't go together. I made mistakes I couldn't turn back from and before I knew it, there was nothing punk about Afro-Punk anymore. I bailed.

With me out of the way, AFROPUNK™ became a corporate international brand, promoting major-label hip-hop and R&B. A new generation of Black punks showed up to the fests and were disappointed to find the few rock acts hidden on a stage no one could find. AFROPUNK™ did nothing to support the needs of Afro-Punks. Cries of co-opting of culture were drowned out by clickbait featuring fabulously costumed concertgoers. Once again, the angry underground took to action. Kids from all over the country stuck their middle fingers high into the air pointing directly toward AFROPUNK™.

The underground needs the mainstream only so far as it needs something to react against. That new generation of active Black punks went on to start their own festivals, collectives, and conversations. That is where this book *Black Punk Now* centers itself. Some of the people I met while making the film are represented. Cartoonist Joanna Davis-McElligatt memorializes her brother Matt, the scene maker from Iowa. Laina Dawes interviews the Black women who made up the Sista Grrrl Riot. Hacktivist Matt Mitchell talks ones and zeros with Ashaki M. Jackson. A younger group of writers, comic creators, and band leaders continue the conversation that my documentary *Afro-Punk* started.

To read this collection of essays, stories, interviews, and comics from the "After *Afro-Punk*" generation is a blessing. No longer alone, I'm proud to call these folks my family.

James Spooner
October 2022

Beyond Bad Brains

HAD TO GAMBLE ON MUSIC IN JUNIOR HIGH, SPENDING MY BIRTHDAY money on the cheapest releases by the punk bands I'd spied on other skaters' shirts.

The safest bet was usually an EP; a few songs for a few bucks. It didn't always pay off (the less that's said about that slow Black Flag joint, the better), but when it did, it was more than a game changer . . . it was a life changer.

I hit the jackpot with *Spirit Electricity* by Bad Brains, six songs for $4.99, at the strip-mall record store by the soup-and-salad spot that my mom loved. Bad Brains had stopped me in my tracks when I saw them in *Thrasher*. A Black band credited with taking punk to the next level? I had to hear it.

I grew up with a Hendrix and Thin Lizzy–loving Black father but was quickly learning that being Black and liking hard guitar music were mutually exclusive outside our house in early '90s Boston. *Spirit Electricity* let me bring a feeling of home with me as I set out on my skateboard. Bad Brains showed me that I could be me, and I put "Let Me Help" on dozens of mixtapes for new friends, hoping that this lightning-fast Black punk band would provide me context as I rolled through my 'burb with an Afro pick in my hoodie pocket.

My family moved to Richmond, Virginia. As I started going

to DIY shows, I learned about Poly Styrene from X-Ray Spex and Bubba Dupree from Void and even met a handful of other young Black punks. Still, I was having a hard time reconciling my Blackness with my punkness. I wished there was more out there. It still felt like you could be Bad Brains, or you could be white.

Even today, when I talk about Black punk, Bad Brains are the first name that people mention. They deserve it. They are the first and best hardcore punk band. Music they released forty years ago still gets me so amped that my pits start to stink when I hear it. But, while I've been busy with *Spirit Electricity*, exciting new music and art has been appearing, and I was really glad to use this book as a chance to get caught up and share a bunch of it here.

A goal of *Black Punk Now* is to give punks—especially the Black ones—a wider frame of reference; to show all of the strains, styles, and identities of Black punk that are thriving; and give newcomers to the scene more chances to see themselves.

So, when James and I say, "Beyond Bad Brains," we're talking about world-stretching fiction like Mariah Stovall's feminist fairy tale "The Princess and the Pit" and the queer collective-house sci-fi of Alex Smith's "Smoke Again, Akhi."

We mean calls to action like golden sunrise collier's how-to, "Big Takeover: Zines as a Freedom Technology for Black Punks and Other Marginalized Groups."

And, since punk isn't punk without righteous, innovative music, we're spending time with life-affirming newer bands like Soul Glo, whose singer Pierce Jordan does a deep dive on the lyrics to their song "Jump!! (Or Get Jumped!!!)((by the future))"; and Rough Francis, whose frontperson Bobby Hackney Jr. shares the story of discovering his own father's proto-punk past in "Punk Family Business."

When we were first talking to Soft Skull Press about doing *Black Punk Now*, they asked if we could define Black punk. We said it's punk by Black people, and that can mean a lot of things. While there are common themes and threads that wind throughout this book—like liberation, community, and inheritance—the modes of expression and points of view are as varied as the Black people who share them. The pieces in *Black Punk Now* work together to create a big picture, a holistic definition of Black punk where every piece stands on level ground.

And if you're a kid with a pick in your hoodie pocket, plus some cash from your aunt and a list of punk bands you want to hear, this book is for you. I hope you see your future self in these pages.

Chris L. Terry
October 2022

NO WHITES ON THE MIC

ROUNDTABLE

WHAT ADJECTIVES WOULD
YOU USE TO DESCRIBE BLACK PUNK?

A ROUNDTABLE DISCUSSION BETWEEN
THE FEMME ORGANIZERS OF NEW
BLACK AND BROWN
PUNK FESTIVALS

*INTERVIEW CONDUCTED BY
SAMM SAXBY FOR
SOFT SKULL PRESS*

*EDITED FOR LENGTH AND
CLARITY BY JAMES SPOONER
AND CHRIS L. TERRY*

CHRISTINA LONG - #BLKGRLSWURLD

First one is "necessary." The second is "liberating," and the third is a phrase: "We don't die, we multiply."

SHAWNA SHAWNTÉ - 143RD DIMENSION (FORMERLY THE MULTIVRS IS ILLUMINATED)

I would say "subversive." In that, it is meant to be subversive, not a trend or a fashion statement.

SCOUT CARTAGENA - BREAK FREE FEST

"Warm" is a word I like to use to think about us. And then I say, "resilient." "Wild."

COURTNEY LONG - #BLKGRLSWURLD

Oh, I would say "magical." I just think it's cool; all the different ideas people come up with when there's no boundaries. When there's no box.

Then "powerful" and "confident." It takes a lot of guts to go someplace knowing you're the only one and not caring, just having a good time. It's so freeing.

SHANNA COLLINS - BLACK BROWN INDIGENOUS CREW

"Aggressive," "hostile," but also "compassionate."

MONIKA ESTRELLA NEGRA - BLACK AND BROWN PUNK COLLECTIVE

"Transformative." Black punks have been the blueprint for fusing music and art with political praxis. As a Black person, every day is political, and everything that you touch is political. There's a moment of clarity that happens when Black punks are talking about issues that affect people within subcultural spaces.

"Revolutionary" can go in tandem with that.

"Audacious," having the audacity to call people out, specifically white punks who want to speak the lingo, but not necessarily apply that ideology to their everyday lives.

STEPHANIE PHILLIPS - DECOLONISE FEST

"Revolutionary." "Necessary." And also "Freeing."

The thing that keeps me in the punk scene and keeps me wanting to make music is that it completely changed my life and made me see things in a different way. Growing up as a Black girl in the UK, society's idea for you and what you should be is very limited. And punk in itself is something where you can be whatever you want to be and break free from any constraints.

BIPOC FESTS

Scenes ebb and flow, festivals come and go. The community is ours to make. These folks took it upon themselves to run collectives and put on shows that reflect their needs. You can too!

For inspiration, check out all these POC-focused festivals and collectives, some defunct, some still happening.

- Oakland/San Francisco - 143rd Dimension (formerly the Multivrs Is Illuminated)
- San Antonio - Xicanas in the Pit
- Houston - Black Brown Fest
- Chicago - Black, Brown and Indigenous Crew/...Or Does It Explode (fest)
- Atlanta - Punk Black
- Philadelphia - Break Free Fest
- New York - #Blkgrlswurld
- New York - Sista Grrrl Riot
- London - Decolonise Fest
- Berlin - Decolonoize Fest

THE PRINCESS AND THE PIT

FICTION

MARIAH STOVALL

"Thinking about why I had such long hair for such a long time even though it was really incompatible with being in a pit reminded me of the fact that beauty standards are mythical. They're fake things with real social consequences."

THE WITCH FINDS HER IN SWEET SOIL BY THE RIVER AND FIGURES, why not? She shushes her cries and listens for footsteps on the wind. All's quiet. She must be royal, per the cloth she's swaddled in. Discarded for not being a son. The Witch scoffs. She prefers sweet girls. She rubs the keloid on her chin twice for good luck, scoops the babe into her arms and calls her Rapunxel. If she squints, she can see her own face in the child's. A new face, however familiar, is welcomed by the lonely. The Witch has been in exile for so long and for such hazy reasons that her reputation as revered, if feared, has crumbled. The new generation of humans thinks her harmless if they believe in her at all. As new magics, more mechanical than hers, arrived, the village lands sprawled toward industry, pushing old ways and old women to the outskirts. Before the oracles scattered into hiding, they told of a spiderwoman with many faces who will one day rain havoc on the tidy, shining world. Until then, the Witch has the babe to keep busy. The forest gives them everything they need. They never venture outside the thicket.

Xel grows grand and beautiful in flesh and in spirit, and short on brains. The Witch teaches her to press oils from the fruits and nuts on the bushes. Together, they work them into Xel's hair every evening. Her hair coils in every direction and puffs like clouds, thick as the loudest clap of thunder and dark as beetle shells in the night. The only time Xel sits still is when they detangle it each dawn. The Witch tries not to worry that Xel isn't interested in the practical arts of stitching hides and starting fires. Instead, Xel imitates the animals' calls for hours on end. She loves the predators' growls most of all. She wishes they'd come closer and she's not sure if she would run to them or from them, only that it'd be an honor to face them. But they never come close, because the Witch's magic makes their camp safe for all the little birds.

Would you like to try singing like the things with feathers, the

Witch asks one afternoon. Xel laughs and carries on her favorite dance: climbing to the top of the canopy of trees and jumping into a heap of leaves. Then she springs to her feet and slams back and forth between the tree trunks that grow in a perfect circle, shouting all the while. Xel's throat blisters and her skin stings with scrapes. The Witch harvests honey and smears a salve on to soothe her. Xel never scars. She stays beautiful.

Xel grows bigger and her hair grows longer. The Witch forgets the prophecy of the spiderwoman, and no longer wonders if the goddess will be friend or foe. She gets sick with a new worry. What if Xel's hair catches on twig or thorn and her lovely neck snaps in half! She'd warn Xel to be careful, but she loves her too much to interrupt her snarling and slamdancing. Xel probably wouldn't hear her anyway. The Witch wipes her tears and whispers a secret spell, rubbing the keloid on her chin thrice to cast it. From this day on, Xel's hair will never hurt her, so long as Xel protects it at all costs. Most importantly, she must never cut it, not even an inch.

By the time Xel is thirteen, the woods are changing. The plants shrivel. The animals disappear and Xel has only her own howls to remember them by. Gone too are the Witch's favorite warblers. Little by little, the wise woman loses faith in all that she knows. Will we vanish too, Xel asks. The Witch was once certain that a prince would come whisk Xel away to a life of safety and spoils. Now the Witch only mentions true love and happily ever after in passing. If the girl's fortune does change, at least she will have her hair. With it, any prince will be easy to entangle.

Love is not in the air when Xel sees another human for the first time. She makes a wretched noise like death. The Witch turns her tongue strangely sharp, warning Xel to be quiet. The foreign man is intent to ravish and remake the forest, the beaches on the coast, the world beyond. Who knows what he might do to a simple princess. The Witch begs Xel to stop carrying on. Is she trying to get caught and captured? It's no use. Xel cannot comprehend so much at once. She stays screeching, rightly terrified though ignorant of what's at stake. The Witch sighs and shoves a tincture down her throat.

Xel wakes up alone. The wooden panels beneath her feet are nothing like trees. The concrete walls around her are nothing like rocky cliffs. The bulb in the ceiling is nothing like a star. She shrieks every sound she knows. No one returns her calls. The Witch appears at random, with food and water and oils for her hair. Xel asks when they can go home. The Witch shakes her head, her eyes so empty that even Xel understands her gloom is too deep to probe. The Witch opens her mouth. She croaks a note of keening defeat before she rubs her keloid and poofs into thin air. This prison has neither door nor window. Xel forgets the forest altogether, but never the Witch who loved the land, perhaps more than she loved her child.

The years drag on and break her. Xel wishes for death. She dreams of it every day, until one night, a familiar roar rouses her from deep sleep. Is the forest so near? She listens closer. No, this is a new sound, coming from below her. She rolls out of bed and pushes her cot to the side to investigate. Just then, a hole rips open in her floor. She gasps and lowers her head to the portal. Brightness is falling from it. The torch is in the hand of a man with no hair. He lands in a sea of similar creatures, on a floor many feet below hers. Xel is relieved not to see him hurt. She didn't get the best look at him, but the bald light-bearer is the most beautiful man she can imagine. After the man in the forest, he is the second man she has ever seen.

A song loud and fast shoots up through the hole. These aren't animal sounds at all. These are people sounds, like the ones she used to make in the wild. The scene many feet below her is dim but she spots dozens of people making noise at each other. Most use only their voices. Some pluck and pound tools to make rhythms and melodies. She goes faint with excitement. Everything goes black. As she rolls onto her side, unconscious, her hair tumbles through the hole, its ends hanging just above the floor of the room below hers.

She wakes to a tug on her neck. Something is scaling her mane, but whatever it is feels strangely weightless. She carefully sits up and the bald man hoists himself into her cot. Her body vibrates, though she can't name why she feels nervous to be near him. Up close, he isn't bald at all! Very short hair, crow-colored like hers, grows from his scalp. He smiles at her and says he has never seen a girl so fine or hair so long. He asks her to promise him she'll never cut it. She laughs at the strange sequence of words. What does it mean to cut your hair, she asks, and he laughs back at her. He explains that most people cut their hair many times in life. He does it every two weeks. Her jaw drops. The Witch never taught her that! Xel is grateful for this new, better teacher.

Akwasi loves answering Xel's questions about the world underground. She loves his stories about something called punk and chandelier-swinging over mosh pits. He is gentle with her in a way he has never been with another. He never mocks her not knowing. He says he could spend his life by her side, tracing the length of her hair, finding the right words to unfurrow her brow when the most basic concept—telephones; penguins—confounds her. She asks him if they will be together forever. This is the thing the Witch could not give her, though Xel holds a secret hope that they will live together again as mother and daughter, even if not in the forest. Akwasi promises to build Xel a palace fit for a princess. She still isn't sure what a princess is, but doesn't want to interrupt his castle-related ramblings. We are in true love, she thinks, her eyes drooping closed. When the sun starts to rise, he tosses her hair back into the hole and prepares to climb away. She cries until he pledges to return. He hands her a piece of paper covered in symbols and assures her that he'll be back—there will be another show underground soon. She believes him. The Witch didn't teach her how to read.

The week without him is long, but she hears his call eventually. Xel, he yells, Xel, what's good with that good hair? She can't lower her ladder fast enough. Soon he is in her cot again, dazzling her with his mundane tales of everyday life in the city. He tells her exactly how many minutes late his bus was last week, and how few empty seats there were when it finally arrived, but not where it was taking him or why he had been so eager to get there. Then he asks if she'd like to come down to the underground tonight. She wants nothing more, but how will she get back up? She must be home for the Witch's next visit, whenever it may be! And doesn't he want to meet her family? Akwasi tells her not to worry, not to get too ahead of herself. He jumps through the hole first and lands on his feet. She takes a leap of faith after him.

The underground is stunning. She never knew there were others like her—unwashed and aggressive. No one bats an eye at her skimpy dress made from animal hide. If only the Witch could see her now. But when she joins her new tribe's dance, her hair catches on everything. It snags in zippers and threads through large holes in people's ears. It gets trampled. Accidentally licked. Sweat soaked. It's going to take a lot of oil to fix. The Witch can't see her like this! As soon as the show is over, Xel begs Akwasi to help her get back to the overground. He and his friends form a human pyramid for her to stumble up. They don't bother looking for a staircase or anything, because something weird is clearly going on with this girl. They told Akwasi not to get involved. He is known to fall in and out of love with ease. His breakups are notoriously ugly; vandalism, indelible insults, and public disturbances abound. Xel will not be able to handle the inevitable.

Xel knows none of this. Every few nights, she heeds his call. He comes up to touch her and be touched by her before they descend. She knows the Witch wouldn't approve, but where is she, anyway? Why did she leave before telling Xel exactly what to do with her body, or Akwasi's, in times like these? Xel knows something of how the animals mated in the forest, but she doesn't have the whole picture. Akwasi gives directions when she stalls and something like sloppy magic sparks between them. It never lasts long, though. He's so excited to touch her; she's impatient for what waits below.

Sometimes the same groups perform. Sometimes there are new ones from faraway places, who, like Xel, are only visiting the underground. Akwasi introduces her to everyone with pride. Then he lets her fall to the periphery of every confusing conversation between sets. During the music, he tries to make her wear earplugs, but she goes so hard in the pit that they fall out every time. She whips her head, her hair, faster and faster, not caring what it catches in its path. She skanks and stagedives and doesn't feel the strands she sheds all over the venue, nor does she notice everyone's glares, because waist-length locs and mile-high mohawks are fine, but they have to draw the line somewhere.

A new band is on stage tonight. One of the women in it barks into her microphone, egging on the crowd. She says she wants to see some-one die tonight. What a wonderfully strange thing to say! Xel pushes closer to the woman, who removes her leopard-skin cap to wipe the sweat from her brow. Xel cannot believe her eyes. The woman is bald, her hair shorter even than Akwasi's. She's gorgeous and glittering. Oh imagine, Xel thinks, how much easier my life in the underground would be if I didn't have all this hair. As soon as the woman's set is over, Xel tells her how marvelous her not-hair is. Nancy says, with a twinkle in her eyes, that Xel could rock a shaved head too. She strong-arms her into the bathroom and pulls out a switchblade. Xel can't believe her luck. Nancy coos and cackles at Xel's innocence and hacks at her hair with a tenderness that makes Xel miss the Witch. Xel feels so sentimental that she stuffs her locks into her pockets. She smiles at her new reflection in the glass above the sink.

After the headliner's set, Xel is talking shit with Nancy and her friends when Akwasi pulls her away midsentence. Something flashes in his eyes. Xel looks around in a panic. It's Akwasi's crew as far as the eye can see. The looks on their faces tell her not to scream for help. Akwasi pulls her closer and says he's not mad, just disap-pointed. She promised never to cut her hair. How could she be so selfish? Why should his friends help her busted ass back up to her castle now? Good luck getting home, they tell her. The underground is empty. Lights off, air wet and rotten. She asks Akwasi why they can't go to his castle instead. He throws his head back and cackles with rage. This is not like the anger on the stage or in the pit. She trembles. The Witch appears. A whiff of herbs. And black.

Xel is in her cell. The Witch is weeping, the keloid gone from her chin. She made the protection spell in Xel's hair so strong that her powers have been in decline ever since. And Xel has made it all for nothing. Xel demands a new spell, to turn back time, anything to fix it. The Witch dries her tears and sighs. Though she loves Xel very much, this is goodbye. Xel gears up to throw the tantrum of the century, but nothing can stop what's already in motion. The Witch must return to what's left of the forest so her spirit may rest. She says it is best for Xel to live out her life in the city. The tepid abandonment ignites endless sorrow. Xel's affection for the Witch, she realizes, is the truest of loves. She wishes the Witch would scold her, and feel for herself the beauty of releasing rage. Xel opens her mouth to beg the Witch to lash out at her, but poof. Alone again!

Xel falls to her cot with such force that the hair she'd stuffed in her pockets spills out. She never asked for the Witch to waste her power protecting her and her hair. What good is beauty when she's only just had her first glimpse of a graffitied mirror? Well, the Witch may be gone but Xel might be able to win back Akwasi. Perhaps he only loved her for her hair, but perhaps she only loved him for his promise to stay. She weaves what she can into a wig, sticks it to her scalp with the strongest salve she can concoct, then sobs herself comatose. Maybe she's just as powerful as the Witch. More, even. Xel is the one who floats over danger, who dances with the dark. She will never be alone again.

Some moons later, she wakes to a kiss. Akwasi has climbed up her hair without asking permission. If this is what she wanted, why do her insides ache? His tongue ring clicks against her teeth. She wants to bite down. But the Witch is gone and Xel didn't get Nancy's number, not that Xel even has a phone. She only has Akwasi. He softens for a second, but as soon as her hastily made wig slips off-kilter, the anger switches on in him again. She apologizes and makes a new promise: her hair will grow back before he knows it. The Witch always brings her the best oils in the land. She'll be beautiful in no time, she swears. Xel has never lied before. She thinks she likes it.

Akwasi comes and goes as he pleases, checking her paltry hair growth each time, clicking his tongue to scold her. Lying isn't fun when she gets caught. She doesn't bother asking to go underground. She asks silly questions about the world, ones she can already answer, trying to rekindle what they once had. He grunts at her bad memory and her bare, empty skull. She wrests a kiss from him and gets the funny feeling that she's being watched. When she pulls away, his lips are lax and his eyes are growing. He gawks at the crown of her head. When he leaves that night, he does not return. She cannot bear it. Even worse is her body's cruel new joke: the heavier her heart, the more hurried her hair growth. Now it springs forth so fast it hurts. But it's too late. Akwasi's not here to see it, the Witch not there to preen it. Xel rips it out at the roots. The tangled mass of it drifts through the hole. There hasn't been a show in weeks. Soon she wakes to find the floor repaired. Her world is so small again. Her hair grows on.

One day, after the earth has made a full circle round the sun, and Akwasi and the Witch are still missing, the rumbling sound returns. Xel stomps at the space where the hole once was, until she falls right through, her unstoppable mane hanging long once again. She lands on the old strands of hair she'd shed and tossed away before. It's just like the leaves that caught her in the forest all those years ago. Someone pulls her up to her feet and hugs her tight. Nancy! She explains that her band Anansi is back in town on tour and that the venue just reopened, under a new collective's management. Last year, Akwasi's crew apparently fell behind on rent and crowdfunded the money to save the space, only to give up and pocket everything when they couldn't decide whose name to put on the new lease. The merry landlord refused to rent it to anyone else out of spite, until now. Xel nods at Nancy's news, in awe of her new teacher.

Something is different about Nancy. Xel can't put her finger on it and she doesn't want to hurt herself thinking too hard. She just wants the show to start. But they're running two hours behind schedule, inexplicably. While they wait, Nancy teaches Xel how to braid the mountain of her hair that's taking up half the venue. Why didn't the Witch teach her this? Xel scratches and bruises herself trying to keep up with Nancy's nimble fingers. They weave it into an unbreakable rope in time with someone's fifth sound check. Then Nancy lowers her voice. She says she has a plan to teach Akwasi a lesson for breaking his promise. Xel leans in and nods along. Finally, the fun begins.

Nancy is shredding on stage and Xel can't take her eyes off her. Of course! It's Nancy's hair that's different. It's now ten inches long, blade-of-grass straight, palm-leaf green. But how? Is she a witch too? Akwasi taught her about cutting hair, but not about changing the hues and shapes of the strands. Xel smacks herself. She must focus. It's almost time . . . During the breakdown, Nancy gives the signal. Xel lifts the rope from where they hid it under Nancy's amp. Everyone is wilding out. The crowd is the perfect cover. Xel finds Akwasi in the pit and slips the braid around his neck once, twice, thrice. She pulls it tight. Indigo blushes his cheeks and he falls. When the dust settles and the crowd clears, she and Nancy add their fake screams to the real ones. Akwasi isn't getting up! No one knows what to do. Can he afford to go to the hospital? Can it wait until after the encore? Is he worth saving? Xel helps Nancy and the rest of Anansi pack up their gear. She climbs in their van, imagining the look on Akwasi's face when he wakes up and realizes she's gone, the desperation in his eyes when he tracks her down and begs for her back, the span of his smile when she says yes.

The strange restraint of a seat belt makes her squirm, but her heart soon stops pounding. Trees blur on the other side of the windows. Xel can never return to the forest. She can't fend for herself and the Witch is a distant memory. She turns to Nancy and asks her the question gnawing at her guts. How did she change her hair so completely? Nancy pats Xel's head and smiles. She shows her hundreds of pictures of people with bark-brown skin like theirs, and hair in just as many shapes and shades and sizes and styles. Xel doesn't believe it's true—that you can make your hair whatever, whenever, and then something new altogether, over and over again, forever. Nancy swears the people in the pictures are real. She's Xel's best teacher by far.

Xel knows everyone must be tired of her questions, but there's one more thing on her mind. She asks, What's Anansi? The band takes turns telling their favorite stories about the sly spider. When the tales run out, the stars above have come and gone. Who do y'all trick then? Xel asks. The van goes faster toward the dawn. The locks click shut. Before anyone can answer her, she screams and shakes the trees. The bassist swerves into the other lane. Nancy rolls her eyes and reaches over to turn the steering wheel away from the highway divider. They trick anyone and everyone, the drummer explains. They thrive on chaos because they can. Once they're smooth sailing again, Nancy climbs into the gutted backseat. She cradles Xel and hushes her wailing. The princess looks up and wipes her snot on the back of her hand. My prince is dead, she whimpers. Akwasi's not just sleeping! You're a monster, she growls at Nancy. So are you, Nancy winks. You're welcome.

TOUGH GUY

COMIC

AYTI KRALI

"In our Virginia scene back in the day, I might have summed myself up as the Black, nerdy hardcore kid."

OF COURSE WE ALL KNOW THERE'S **NOTHING MONOLITHIC** ABOUT REAL BLACKNESS. THERE WERE NO WRITTEN RULES, BUT (I BELIEVED) THERE WERE **BOUNDARIES.** AT BEST, EVAN and I WERE ON the **FRINGES.**

THIS COULD HAVE LED TO AN **ALLIANCE.**

Hey, lend me your towel. I just need to wipe my eye.

...BUT IT **DIDN'T.**

HE DIDN'T LIKE ME EITHER...

Here ya go.

FRINGES OR NOT, HE WAS ON the **INSIDE.**

BARELY.

I WAS NOT.

MAYBE WE BOTH SAW THINGS WE DIDN'T LIKE ABOUT **OURSELVES** IN **THE OTHER.** I DON'T KNOW.

BUT WHY WAS HIS ODDNESS **FREE OF CONSEQUENCES** WHY DID I GET CALLED OUT ON MINE?

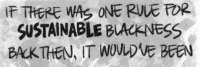
IF THERE WAS ONE RULE FOR **SUSTAINABLE** BLACKNESS BACK THEN, IT WOULD'VE BEEN

PROBABLY BECAUSE ALONG WITH MY OTHER QUIRKS, I **CRIED A LOT.** MOST PEOPLE TOOK THIS FOR **WEAKNESS.** LONE, WEAK, BLACK KIDS SENT the JUNIOR VARSITY KLAN INTO A FEEDING FRENZY.

EVAN and HIS mom **MOVED AWAY** BEFORE JUNIOR HIGH.

WITH HIM OUT OF THE PICTURE, I STUCK OUT EVEN MORE.

VVRMMM

THE COMMUNITY TOOK NOTICE and TRIED TO TOUGHEN ME UP. IT DIDN'T WORK. I CONTINUED TO CRY PUBLICLY, SHAMEFULLY, **CONSTANTLY.** DURING TESTS, AT TRACK PRACTICE... WELL INTO HIGH SCHOOL. OFTEN WOEFUL, CONVULSING SOBS. I WAS REALLY SELF-CONSCIOUS ABOUT THIS.

IT WASN'T PRETTY

STILL, I MADE SOME FRIENDS WHO DIDN'T MIND, CARRIE and DAVE. WE WATCHED 120 MINUTES ON VHS AFTER SCHOOL. I SUFFERED THROUGH R.E.M. JUST TO BE THERE.

AT SOME POINT THOUGH, I SAW **I AGAINST I.** WOEFUL BUT also RAGING and **NOT WEAK.**

THE MESSAGE SHOULD HAVE BEEN "THERE IS POWER IN EXPRESSING **EMOTIONAL VULNERABILITY**" BUT AT 16, ALL I KNEW WAS I NEEDED MORE OF THAT... SO WHEN I MOVED TO THE CITY AT 17, I FOUND the HARDCORE KIDS.

THEY WERE LIKE MY FRIENDS BACK HOME, BUT... INTENSE. and RADICAL and TOUGH.

I WENT WITH THEM TO SEE **BURN** AT A CHURCH IN D.C. CHAKA GROWLED, MATTER OF FACT :

"I'm drowning in a sea of emotion. Drowning."

I WANTED TO EXPRESS MYSELF LIKE **THAT**-- INSTEAD OF CRYING.

IN A PERFECT WORLD SOMEONE WOULD HAVE HAD ME READ **TONI MORRISON** or **ALICE WALKER** FIRST. BUT I FOUND MYSELF IN HARDCORE PUNK and the TEARS STOPPED... **MOSTLY***

INTERLUDE

*SO I WAS IN A BAND and OUR GUITARIST LEFT TO PLAY BASS FOR A SUPER POPULAR LOCAL PUNK BAND. I WASN'T MAD AT HIM. WHO COULD BLAME HIM? THEY TOURED the WORLD. I WAS MAD AT THEM.

INEXPLICABLY

I WENT TO THEIR SINGER TO TELL HIM HOW I FELT. WITHIN 30 SECONDS I WAS CRYING and ALL, "HOW COULD YOU!" HE GAVE ME A HUG and SAID BANDS WERE LIKE ANY OTHER RELATIONSHIP. I LEFT THROUGH the BACK DOOR TO AVOID the OTHER GUYS.

I'm drown---

CREEEAK

OF COURSE THEIR DRUMMER and ROADIE WERE COMING IN THAT WAY AT THE SAME TIME. I COULD FEEL THE PITY AS THEY LOOKED AT MY SNOTTY FACE. IT WAS HUMILIATING. NO ONE SAID A WORD.

• end interlude •

I DIDN'T THINK MUCH OF EVAN BEFORE, BUT I APPRECIATED HIM BEING ON the FRINGES. ESPECIALLY SINCE I'D BEEN **INSIDE** FOR A COUPLE OF YEARS. IT WAS the **OPPOSITE** DYNAMIC BACK HOME.

BUT STILL, EVERYBODY ELSE HERE WAS FROM **RVA, D.C.** or the **BEACH**... and THEY SEEMED SO PUT·TOGETHER. DESPITE BEING ACCEPTED, I STILL FELT LIKE SOME WEIRD, LONE HICK.

MY LOOSE BUT LONG·STANDING TIES TO EVAN, A KNOWN REBEL, SHOWED THAT I HAD PEOPLE and A BACKSTORY.

BUT IT WASN'T AN ACTUAL FRIENDSHIP, EVEN THOUGH WE HAD A LOT IN COMMON.

I SAW HIM AROUND JUST A FEW TIMES OVER the NEXT FEW YEARS.

EACH ENCOUNTER WAS A LESSON IN BEING YOURSELF ...UNAPOLOGETICALLY.

NOW I'M LOOKING AT GROWN-UP EVAN.

HE'S THE SAME 8 YEAR OLD KID WHO COULDN'T SIT STILL. IT'S A LOT TOUGHER TO BE THAT KID AT 48.

PRESENT DAY

NOW, I ASSUME THAT EVAN'S "ODDNESS" WAS PROBABLY ADHD and MINE, LIKELY ANXIETY. KIDS LIKE US in the 1980s WERE USUALLY "DIAGNOSED" HARDHEADED (EVAN), LAZY or SOFT (ME).

and BEING BLACK IN AMERICA MAKES IT ALL MORE... COMPLICATED.

THE COMBINATION of ODDNESS and DARK SKIN CAN BE A RED FLAG FOR SOME CONCERNED CITIZENS.

· END of INNER MONOLOGUE ·

Well? Who is he?

Um.

An old friend

Why is your friend... locked up?

mistakes... made by EVERYONE.

Even you?

Yup

BACK THEN, I SPENT TOO MUCH TIME LOOKING FOR ACCEPTANCE. I FORGOT TO BE ACCEPTING OF OTHERS... and MYSELF.

I **DIDN'T** NEED TO STOP CRYING. I NEEDED TO BE **OK WITH IT.**

I WAS FORTUNATE TO HAVE FOUND A PUNK SCENE THAT DIDN'T STIGMATIZE ME FOR MY IDIOSYNCRASIES.

THIER SUPPORT ALLOWED ME TO WORK OUT A LOT OF ISSUES -- BUT **I STILL CRY**

...WHEN IT'S APPROPRIATE

FIN!

NO WHITES ON THE MIC

ROUNDTABLE

WHY BIPOC AS OPPOSED TO

FOCUSING STRICTLY ON BLACK PUNK

During Afro-Punk's origins—from the documentary to the fest—it wanted to promote Black artistry onstage at the exclusion of other people of color. Y'all's festivals and organizations focus on multiverses, experimentation, and inclusion. Will you speak on those seemingly competitive motivations?

SHAWNA

I don't think they're competitive at all. It seems like [Afro-Punk started at] a different time, and I understand. What we created was a reflection of our community, our friendships. It's just a reflection of who we are, and where we are and who our community is.

Also, coming from the space of being a queer punk, there's this other political component, where I have friends across diasporas, and we're all punk, but we're also queer, which is a whole other thing. It's kind of like a recentering.

STEPHANIE

When I first tweeted out, asking if anyone wanted to see a Black punk festival and who they would like to play, it got people interested. People messaged me, saying it would make sense to create a festival for more than just Black people. I thought that made sense because of the realities of UK colonialism. Why we all came to this country and why we're British and why we have an English accent, and why my family are technically from Jamaica, but obviously, not really from

Jamaica. It's all connected to the history of colonialism and slavery. We have different intersecting experiences, and it affects us in different ways. It reminds us that we're all puppets mastered by white supremacy. And that's the real, proper danger in our lives.

MONIKA

I second that, Stephanie. Specifically, between the struggles of Black and Latinx folks in this country. It's all tied to colonialism and slavery and things of that nature. But there are certain social conditionings that seem to keep the two communities from uniting. But also, let's talk about the pertinent anti-Blackness still existing in Latinx communities. So it's like trying to figure out what solidarity can we actually have in order to move forward with our political ideologies, right?

SHANNA

The thing is, if you're still going to have people of color and Black punk bands performing in the same space, I think a central point is still talking about anti-Blackness. In particular with the brown punk spaces in Chicago. We do have people of color here who join in our solidarity, but it's important for them to understand and to critique their own internalized anti-Blackness.

COURTNEY

For us, it's really cool when you find a Pakistani metal band. It's just like, "Why would we want to exclude them from our festival?"

Or BABYMETAL, a Japanese, female-fronted band . . . like, come on, how can we not have this?

SHAWNA

It was very important for us that white people not have microphones. And that the bands were 50 percent Black or POC. I would always joke, "No whites on the mic!" I got a lot of shit for that.

SCOUT

It does take curating. This is obviously a more complicated conversation, but I had someone who was like, "But I'm Jewish!" And I was like, "Okay, this is a conversation that might be outside of my reach. But, let's talk about this. Your band is primarily white, you say you are the leading diversity in this band? Something about that doesn't taste right to me."

COURTNEY

Yeah, I agree with that. We're trying to curate a special cultural moment. Y'all get booked by everybody else. We're saying, "When has everybody been booked, in this one moment, at this one festival, together?"

We're not trying to hurt nobody's feelings, but it's just like, come on, all in one place together? Like this? That's special!

PUNK FAMILY BUSINESS

NONFICTION

BOBBY HACKNEY JR.

AS TOLD TO CHRIS L. TERRY

"Being Black and punk challenges the idea of what people think 'Black' is supposed to be . . . and that is soooooo punk!"

ME AND MY BROTHERS' DISCOVERY OF DEATH HAPPENED MORE organically than a lot of people think. My brother Julian was having a lot of phone conversations with our dad, asking for music advice, and Dad started to plant seeds and feed him vague stories about his band from before we were born.

Our dad was, like, really shy about it. It was weird because he is usually very outgoing. If Bobby Hackney Sr. is in a room, everybody's paying attention to him. He's that type of guy, a Leo.

Julian was intrigued and, every time they spoke, he would pull out a little more info until Dad finally said that the band was called Death, and that they'd released a single in 1974. When Julian searched "Politicians in My Eyes," the only thing that popped up was Ben Blackwell's post on *Chunklet* with the MP3s. When we heard it, we just knew.

We grew up listening to our dad and uncle Dannis play in this reggae band called Lambsbread. They're pretty well-known around New England. So, hearing Death was like taking what we knew of their playing and applying it to rock. It was their style, just a different genre of music.

We were really into punk and we had no idea that our father and uncles used to play it, so we were simply blown away to hear those songs. I had no idea that they were capable of making the music that they made in Death. I was also very surprised that my grandmother let them practice in their shared bedroom. I can only imagine how loud it was.

We asked Dad if there was any more music, and he was like, "Oh, yeah, I have some tapes. Bring them down from the attic and convert them."

I was stunned when I heard all the other songs.

<hr>

One of the better bands I was in when I was younger was this hard-core band called Common Ground. We recorded a seven inch. I was really excited about it and showed my dad, like, "Check it out!"

He was listening to it and said, "Yeah, this reminds me of Black Sabbath a little bit." And I was like, "You know Black Sabbath?!"

Then he said, "Yeah, me and your uncles used to play music kinda like this when we were younger," but he didn't go any further.

I think that the reason he was so hesitant to tell us was because Death was the dream band, but people thought they were weird because they were three Black dudes playing rock in Detroit in the 1970s. Wherever they went, they faced some kind of rejection. He was proud of the music that they made, and the bond that he had with his brothers, but not having any validation made it seem like an embarrassing secret, you know? They were passionate about it and people didn't like it.

But, if you're doing something that other people don't understand and you still decide to do it, that's punk to me. My dad and uncles did this thing that they thought was awesome. A lot of people around them *didn't* think it was awesome, but they still did it anyway. They created something out of nothing and found a way to make things happen on their own.

I started going to punk shows when I was fourteen or fifteen. I was a skater and I became friends with all the punk kids. I grew up in a rural town called Jericho, Vermont. It's a half-hour away from "the big city," Burlington. And that's where I started playing in various punk bands.

My parents were supportive but, honestly, I think they would have been more excited if I joined the basketball team. My mom was always surrounded by musicians, so it was just like, "Time to deal with more band practices and people being late coming home." But I think, deep down, they're proud.

We were making our own demos, and I was recording our music over tapes that we already had. You put Scotch tape over the tabs on a Peter Gabriel tape, or some other random tape from an old shoebox, and you put your own music on it. And after our demo would be done, we'd hear the remainder of whatever we recorded it over. It's not like recycling, but it's making the most of what you have. We didn't wait for anybody to do those things for us, and that taught me a lot. We were young, we had no money, and we figured it out.

ıllıllıllıllıllı

When we first moved out to Jericho, we had this big plot of land that backed onto the elementary school and the middle school. We didn't have a lawnmower at the time, and the grass got really wild and long, so my dad ended up burning it. That was the kind of thing that drew a lot of attention in town because it's like, "Okay, these people move in there and burn the grass?!" But . . . my dad became friends with the fire marshal that day.

We would just be doing things our way and then someone would wonder, *What are these guys doing?* and meet my parents. My parents met all of our friends out there through doing something kinda wacky.

My dad's band Lambsbread would practice at the house. Later, my bands would practice, too. People would be like, "Oh, wow, do I hear music? Oh, that's interesting. You know, we've never heard music out here before." A lot of that.

That's where we grew up, so that became normal to me. And, we were surrounded by some good friends who looked out for us. But the only Black community we had was my family. That was pretty much it. There were a couple other families that moved into town and moved away. And, as soon as there's that new other Black kid at school, everyone's like, "Oh, is that your friend? Is that your brother?"

꙳꙳꙳꙳꙳꙳꙳꙳꙳

After Lambsbread was done with rehearsals, they'd put away the guitars, but my uncle's drums were always there. That's how I learned to play drums. I was always a drummer.

Rough Francis was the first time I became a singer. Learning how to be a frontperson gave me a voice. A lot of the songs that I've written are from the perspective of younger me. I used to keep a lot to myself, and I feel like the band is a perfect vehicle for me to let that stuff out. It's been cathartic.

One of our earlier songs, "Not a Nice Guy," addresses the whole situation of thinking someone was a friend, and then they go behind your back and say and do a bunch of racist stuff. I had to deal with that a lot, so it felt good to let that one out. That really messed me up, you know? I'd thought about that one ever since I was fifteen.

꙳꙳꙳꙳꙳꙳꙳꙳꙳

Finding out about Death was the perfect time for me and my brothers to start our own band, Rough Francis. We thought it was our duty to let people know about our dad and uncles' band, so we started covering their music. It taught us how to be in a band together instead of starting from scratch and trying to figure out our sound.

When Death finally went out on tour, it was cool to see my dad and uncle have the fun that they've always wanted to have. I feel like, to this day, they're still blown away by people liking their music. Because for a while, nobody liked it. Nobody knew about it.

But, once my dad and uncle took those songs out on the road, Rough Francis was like, "Okay, well, what are we going to do?" We started to write our own stuff because we needed to prove ourselves, separate from Death.

Being a Death tribute act was funny, because it's not like we were a tribute to a huge band like Aerosmith. Death get recognition and accolades, but they're not a household name, so it was this really obscure thing.

A lot of bigger bands, when their kids form a band, it's like, "Oh, yeah, you're just big because your dad was in Led Zeppelin." But for us, it's just that one nerd at the record store who knows about us. It's really funny.

We're both part of the story. We're separate, but super interconnected. You can't mention one without the other, and that's what's really cool about it. If anybody knows about us, or Death, it's a win for the whole family.

The Hackney brothers at the legendary Burlington, Vermont, all-ages venue 242 Main in the early 2000s. Pictured left to right: Julian (crouching), Bobby, and Urian. Photographer unknown.

LET ME BE MISUNDERSTOOD

FICTION

KASH ABDULMALIK

"Nobody is
more punk
than the
Black
youth of
America."

J.SPOONER-22

Let Me Be Misunderstood

A Short Film

Written by Kash Abdulmalik

**EXT. A QUIET RESIDENTIAL NEIGHBORHOOD IN
PASADENA - DAY**

We open on a nice, suburban neighborhood shot of
Pasadena mid-day. TALIB ABDUR-RAHMAN (Black, 40)
pulls up in a Prius with "My Dad Sucks" by the
Descendents blasting. He gets out and enters a serene gated apartment building. Carrying a bag of
Popeyes chicken, he takes note of it and then the
viewer. Speaking in a slight New York accent, he
breaks the fourth wall.

> TALIB
> Way to perpetuate a stereotype, right?
> ...It's for my dad. (beat) What?—It is!
> Screw you, you don't know...I'm probably
> only gonna have one piece. Two, tops.
> Speaking of stereotypes, what are some
> for fathers? The ones I'm used to hearing
> are...the telling of dumb dad jokes,
> the dad who is always working on fix-up
> projects around the house with countless
> tools on his belt, or my favorite, the
> father figure who you can always have a
> heart-to-heart with... Yeah. Not my dad.

INT. APARTMENT LOBBY - CONTINUOUS

Talib strolls into the building lobby.

> TALIB
> See, now my dad seemed to follow all the
> other stereotypes out there. You know,
> emotionally unavailable, recklessly
>
>   (MORE)

aggressive, and my most favorite of all, inflexibly controlling. Gotta love that one. I always kinda hoped that one day maybe he'd let his guard down so we could have at least some sort of an honest relationship or just a conversation. Or maybe I've seen too many movies.

INT. APARTMENT ELEVATOR - CONTINUOUS

                    TALIB
As my parents got older I felt the need to move them out to California from our native Brooklyn to help take care of them. Plus, adding insult to injury, my dad now has dementia. Add that to his already cheery disposition and...well, it's a lot. My mother is another story entirely. I won some type of universal lottery with her.

INT. THE ABDUR-RAHMAN PASADENA HOUSEHOLD – CONTINUOUS

The Abdur-Rahman apartment is warm and inviting. HAKIMAH ABDUR-RAHMAN (Black, 78, but you'd never guess by looking at her) sits at the kitchen table on her laptop. A massive Bad Brains sticker adorns the front of it. As Talib enters, she jumps up and gives him an immediate hug and kiss on the cheek. You can hear a loud TV from the rear of the apartment.

                    TALIB
Hey, Ma, how you doing?

HAKIMAH
So much better now that I'm seeing you,
sweetie! Thank you for doing this. He's
been going on and on about the fried
chicken. Nonstop.

TALIB
Ugh, I'm sorry. How's he doing today?

HAKIMAH
He's throwing another fit, but you know
him. It's minute to minute. You can just
drop the food off and leave. I know you're
busy.

TALIB
That's okay, I'll stick around for just
a bit and try to see if I can quell the
beast.

HAKIMAH
Yeah, right.

They exchange a familiar look, she gives him another hug, and then Talib heads down the hallway
toward his father's room. In horror movie fashion,
the floor creaks down the seemingly endless corridor as a light shines from beneath the door of his
father's room. Talib approaches cautiously, sweat
beading on his brow.

Finally, he reaches the door, and extends his hand
to the knob. He's about to turn it—and THEN—fourth
wall again.

                      TALIB
        Hold up. Before we do this, I feel you
        should probably get a glimpse of just
        who my dad and I were before you see who
        we are now. It's kinda necessary for the
        story. Okay? Cool. Let's jump back to 2002
        when my punk band Fatal Flaw was on our
        first East Coast tour.

                                          CUT TO:

EXT. BROOKLYN HEIGHTS, NEW YORK - DAY

A blistering, hot, muggy summer. A van full of
punk rockers pulls up in front of a twelve-story
apartment building as "New Generation" by Zero
Boys plays from the radio.

INT. APARTMENT ELEVATOR - CONTINUOUS

Talib (now in his late 20s with blue hair), DARLA
(white, early 30s) the bassist, CHUCK (Japanese, late
teens) the drummer, and CLINT (white, late 20s) the
guitarist all stand cramped in the small elevator.

                      CLINT
        ...So you grew up in an office building.

                      TALIB
        No, it's New York man, the city is just
        stacked on top of itself. (beat) Actually,
        I think this was an office building in the
        '20s or something.

                      CHUCK
        Crazy. Your mom coming to the show?

                    TALIB
          Can't keep her away.

INT. BROOKLYN APARTMENT HALLWAY - MOMENTS LATER

The band saunters down the hallway to the Abdur-
Rahmans' apartment door.

                    DARLA
          What about your dad and your brother?

                    TALIB
          Yeah... Let's hope not.

                    DARLA
                  (laughing)
          Dude, the way you make 'em sound, I just
          wanna see how they'd react when we go off.
          Like, maybe your dad will try to convert
          the crowd to Islam and your brother will
          try to sell everyone heroin.

                    TALIB
          You make it sound like I've been calling
          them fucking monsters. They're not,
          they're just, y'know...assholes.

Talib knocks on the door as the band chuckles.

                    CLINT
          Come on, man, I'm sure they're not that bad.

A slightly intoxicated FARID ABDUR-RAHMAN (early
30s) opens the door. He gives everyone the once-
over twice.

                                                    53.

                    FARID
Oh shit, whaddup fat boy? These your white
boys from California?

                    CHUCK
...I'm Japanese.

                    DARLA
...Not a guy.

                    FARID
               (to the band)
Yo, this nigga ever tell you about the
time I pissed all over him when he was
sleeping and I was fucked up? Hahaha!
That's punk right?

                    CLINT (TO TALIB)
Wow.

                    TALIB (TO CLINT)
I fucking told you.

                    FARID
Told him what?

                    TALIB
Nothing.

                    FARID
You tell these guys that I'm an asshole,
right?

                    TALIB
Nah, I just—

54.

                    FARID
'Cause that sure sounds like a bitch-made
move of yours.

                    TALIB
                 (deep sigh)
Farid, this is Clint, Chuck, and Darla.
Guys, this is my brother. The "asshole" I
was telling you about.

                    FARID
That's what I thought.

Everyone exchanges an awkward hello with Farid as
the band enters the tiny New York apartment. He's
smaller than Talib and has the presence of a high
school bully. Not threatening, just annoying.

INT. THE ABDUR-RAHMAN HOUSE - CONTINUOUS

As Talib walks the band down the long hallway
of the railroad-style apartment, he quietly rem-
inisces over childhood in the crowded space. He
hears echoes of arguments and yelling matches with
his brother. It's definitely the opposite of its future Pasadena counterpart.

The memories are broken up by the background music
of "The Regulator" by Bad Brains, which emanates
from the kitchen. Hakimah (58) pops her head out
from the kitchen and lets out a tiny squeal of joy.

                    HAKIMAH
Hey, guys! Welcome to Brooklyn!

                              TALIB
              Hi, Mom!

                            THE BAND
              Hi, Mrs. Abdur-Rahman!

                             HAKIMAH
              As many times as I've seen you guys play,
              you better stop with all that formality
              and just call me Hakimah already!

The group smiles and each hug her. Everyone chats
and assembles at the dining room table.

                              CHUCK
              Hakimah, did you buy this album?

                             HAKIMAH
              Oh no, I stole it from Talib.

They all laugh.

                              TALIB
              One way or another, I'm gonna get that
              tape back, Ma.

                             HAKIMAH
                           (giggling)
              Good luck with that! So how has the tour
              been so far?

                              CHUCK
              Almost out of merch, so it's been pretty
              good!

                    CLINT
         Yeah, we played Philly last night, Jersey
         tomorrow, and Rochester the day after.

                    HAKIMAH
         But tonight is my baby's hometown show!

                    DARLA
         And baby is going to perform all of his
         songs about the corrupt government and
         broken society perfectly for his mommy.

Everyone chuckles except for Talib.

                    FARID
         Fake-ass nigga.

                    HAKIMAH (TO FARID)
         Hey, stop that.

This of course sucks all the laughter out of the
room. Then, ENOCH ABDUR-RAHMAN (late 60s) emerges
from his room. Like Darth Vader entering a small
room, judgmental attitude follows him like a bil-
lowing fog.

                    TALIB
         Guys, this is my dad.

With no words and a calm look Enoch quietly shakes
everyone's hands before he finally arrives at his
son. He then looks him up and down.

                    ENOCH
          You pierced your ears. Like a girl.

                    TALIB
          "Hello," Dad.

That's about the most we can expect from him.
Talib shakes his head as his father addresses the
band.

                    ENOCH
          So, any of you Muslim?

The band looks at each other laughingly and then
to Talib.

                    TALIB
          No, Dad, it's, uh...just me.

                    ENOCH
          Okay , that's fine. Any of you have kids?

                    HAKIMAH
          Honey, no. They don't have kids—

                    ENOCH
          Well, when you do, I can help advise you
          how to raise them. I'm a very good father.
          I raised these two boys Muslim and I
          did my best. They haven't killed anyone,
          they're not drunkards, they don't sell
          themselves on the streets, they're not
          faggots, they're—

This strikes Darla hard.

58.

                    DARLA
     Excuse me?

                    TALIB
     —Okay! Thanks, Dad. You don't have to say
     anything else. It's fine. (to Darla) I—I'm
     sorry.

Darla bites her lip and shakes her head. Enoch
walks over to Farid and rests his hand on his
shoulder.

                    ENOCH
     Have you all met Talib's brother, Farid?
     He's my eldest and an amazing artist. Hold
     on, I'll get some of his drawings. You
     should see them. He's very good.

                    FARID
     Thanks, Dad.

As he goes to the other room, Farid throws a middle finger up at his brother behind his mother's
view.

                    HAKIMAH
                    (to Talib)
     Sorry, sweetie.

                    TALIB
     It's okay, Mom. I just wanted to see if
     you wanted to come to the show later.

                    HAKIMAH
     Of course! And I'm bringing your father.

                    TALIB
          No, please. You really don't have to do
          that—

                    HAKIMAH
          He should see you perform at least once.
          Plus you guys are so damned good, I keep
          your CD in my car.

Farid leans over to Darla.

                    FARID
          I thought the music was pretty aight but
          the singer kinda sounds too white. But I
          guess he is by association, right? Hahaha!

                    DARLA
          Talib kinda nailed you with the
          description, didn't he?

Dimly, Farid takes this as a compliment.

                    FARID
          Yeah, he did. I'm just an asshole, what
          can I say? (to Talib) Anyways, I would
          make it to the show but I just can't do
          it, yo. I got some more important stuff in
          the works.

                    TALIB
          Oh, yeah? So, the standard drug deals are
          still being done at night?

60.

                    FARID
     I don't know, are you still a bitch-ass
     nigga who can't keep his mouth shut?

Hakimah snaps at Farid.

                    HAKIMAH
     Hey! Enough with the language, how about
     some respect?

                    FARID
     Sorry, Mama.

Farid walks past his brother, nudging him hard in
the shoulder. The band averts their eyes and tries
to comfort Talib with their gestures.

                    TALIB
     Well, this has been . . . just great.
     We're gonna go get some food, you wanna
     join us, Mom?

                    HAKIMAH
     And leave all this? Absolutely.

Just then Enoch returns holding a book full of ink
drawings and art by Farid.

                    ENOCH
     Wait, you all have to see my son's artwork
     first. These are outstanding.

The band stands around, kindly obliging Enoch as

                                        (MORE)

                                        61.

he brags about his firstborn's artistic achievements. The drawings are actually fantastic. The band looks at them, stifling surprise at how impressive they are.

> CHUCK
> (shocked)
> Wow. These are...really good.

> FARID
> Y'all need to let me draw your next album cover like I've been telling fat boy over here.

> HAKIMAH
> Hey! Enough with that already.

Talib balls his hand into a fist silently. Farid stares at his brother as a smile grows across his face. Knowing his father's praise struck a chord, he basks in it.

After the art show, the band and Hakimah head to the door. Before leaving, Talib looks to his father.

> TALIB
> ...So I guess I'll see you later?

> ENOCH
> I suppose.

Talib rolls his eyes as he walks out.

EXT. HANK'S SALOON MUSIC VENUE - THAT NIGHT

A large murmuring congregation surrounds the two-foot-tall stage. The excitement before the hard-core show is eerie and ominous. The crowd is a mix of young and middle-aged, mostly white rockers. Speckled throughout are a few Black and Brown faces. In the back of the room Hakimah smiles as Enoch notices the diversity.

Friends of Talib and NYHC kids start bashing into each other as "Bad Attitude" by Articles of Faith plays over the loudspeaker. Fatal Flaw walks onto the stage to scattered applause and sound checks in a matter of seconds.

> TALIB
>
> Fuck, man. It's so goddamned humid.

> CLINT
>
> Shouldn't you be used to it? Wasn't it like this growing up here?

> TALIB
>
> It must've been. I think I just got used to the California weather cause this is a fucking sauna.

> DARLA
>
> I get why everyone is walking around with a washcloth now.

Talib grabs the mic as a shitty amplifier rings

(MORE)

out. Across the room, Hakimah waits eagerly for her son to do his thing while Enoch makes a face of disgust as a bald-headed woman passes him while chugging a 40-ounce.

> TALIB
> What's up, we're Fatal Flaw from Los Angeles! It's good to be home, Brooklyn, but now—*I LIVE IN HOLLYWOOD!*

Fatal Flaw dive-bombs into their song about the drug-addled and disgusting streets of Hollywood, and annihilates the crowd. It's fast and snotty, very much a throwback to the California hardcore of the 1980s. Throwing himself into the air and then to the floor, Talib writhes around, shrieking out the lyrics. The crowd storms the stage and start a circle pit. It's exactly the reception Talib was hoping for.

Mid-set, Talib notices his father going outside and not returning. This enrages him as he performs even more maniacally. As he does, the band plays tighter and the crowd goes apeshit. The entire set is blasted through in under twenty minutes.

Hakimah stands further back because the front of the room is full of kids slamdancing. The set ends and the band chats with all their East Coast buddies. A drenched Talib walks over to his mother and gives her a hug.

                              HAKIMAH
           You guys were amazing, as usual!

                              TALIB
                           (chuckles)
           Thanks, Mom, I really appreciate you
           coming. (beat) Where'd, uh, he go?

                              HAKIMAH
           He went outside 'cause he said his ears
           were ringing too much. He had earplugs in
           though... I don't know how—

           She realizes her husband's lack of interest as she
           says it.

                          HAKIMAH (CONT'D)
           I—I'm sorry, I shouldn't have brought him—

                              TALIB
           Nah, it's okay! Honestly, I'm shocked he
           stuck around as long as he did. Tell
           you what, why don't you get a Coke or
           something from the bar, I'm gonna see if
           he's outside still.

                              HAKIMAH
           You don't have to talk to him, hun.

                              TALIB
           It's okay. I want to.

           Talib goes outside, lights a cigarette, and turns

                                              (MORE)

                                                   65.

to see his father. Enoch stands outside in the cold, silent.

                    TALIB (CONT'D)
          Hey, Dad. What'd you think of the show?

                    ENOCH
          I'm sure it was good for what it was.

                    TALIB
          For what it was? Jesus...

                    ENOCH
          WHO?!

                    TALIB
          Nothing.

Beat.

                    ENOCH
          Did I do this? Am I responsible for all of
          that in there? Is it my fault?

                    TALIB
          You're acting like I raped someone or
          something, I'm not a convict. I'm in a
          punk band. It's not—

                    ENOCH
          —It's not the path for a Muslim. Your
          brother, as many problems as he has, still
          follows the tenets of Islam.

                    TALIB
Why are you even talking about him? He's
a fucking drunk, Dad! I can't see how you
can let that go and ride my ass for this!
That's hypocritical bullshit!

                    ENOCH
Don't you dare speak that way to me, I'm
your father!

                    TALIB
You're not even listening to what I'm
saying! Come on... Can we finally have
an honest conversation or is that
impossible?

                    ENOCH
Can you control your language?

                    TALIB
Is that more fucking important than what
I have to say?

Enoch starts to walk away.

                    ENOCH
I'm not doing this with you.

Talib tosses his cigarette into the street, then
heads back to the club.

                                    BACK TO:

INT. THE ABDUR-RAHMAN PASADENA HOUSEHOLD - DAY

We return to a 40-year-old Talib standing at his father's door talking to the viewer.

> TALIB
>
> That was twenty years ago. (sigh) Growing up as a Black punk and being Muslim, I always expected my biggest hurdles to be from the outside, but this was one of the memories that stuck with me the most. My dad never saw me play again or asked about us, and that sucks...but what can you do? The illest part of all this is now I'm the one taking care of him.

Talib opens the door to Enoch's room.

INT. ENOCH ABDUR-RAHMAN'S BEDROOM - CONTINUOUS

The manic eyes of ENOCH (83) light up as he sees his son. The room can only be described as organized clutter. The walls are covered with paintings and drawings of his own making. Framed photos of jazz musicians and relatives fill in the blank spaces. Enoch sits in his chair in the middle of piles of books and makeshift shelves. Both the television and radio are blasting.

> TALIB
>
> Hey, Dad! The TV is pretty loud, I gotta turn it down a little, okay? I can hear it from the elevator!

Talib lowers the volume on the TV.

Beat.

                    ENOCH
         I need some magazines.

                    TALIB
         "Hello," Dad.

                    ENOCH
         Did you hear what I said? I need some
         magazines.

                    TALIB
         What kind of magazines? I just got you
         some yesterday.

                    ENOCH
         Not those kind of magazines. I need
         some...nasty magazines.

                    TALIB
         Dad, no. I'm not buying you porn.

                    ENOCH
         Allah said a child is supposed to hear his
         father's word as law. You have to get me
         what I ask for when I ask for it.

                    TALIB
         I'm pretty sure evoking the words of the
         Quran wasn't meant to get...whatever you're
         into. Ugh.

                    ENOCH
Do you want to know what I'm into?

                    TALIB
I'm guessing it's not guys, right?

Enoch immediately becomes enraged.

                    ENOCH
I'm no faggot! I'm a mud Marine and I want
a fuck book now!

                    TALIB
Okay, okay! I'm sorry. I was just kidding.
Look, I got you some chicken. You're
hungry, right?

                    ENOCH
I DON'T WANT NUTHIN'! I HATE THIS FUCKIN'
PLACE! I WISH I WAS FUCKIN' DEAD!

                    TALIB
Dad, please calm down. Look, Mom told me
you wanted some Popeyes chicken, so I got
you some. It smells good, doesn't it?

                    ENOCH
Leave it and get the fuck out!

                    TALIB
              (deep sigh)
Fine. I'll leave you alone.

Talib puts the bag down and exits the room. As soon as he closes the door, his father yells out—

                    ENOCH
          TAALLIIIIIIIB!

Talib gives a look of tempered annoyance to the camera, bites his lip, and goes back in the room. Still in his comfy chair, Enoch, now with an entirely different attitude, produces a small homemade book of Post-its with notes scribbled on them.

                    ENOCH (CONT'D)
          This is a list of stuff I want.

The lists range from fast food restaurants, to sizes of wooden planks, to styles of pens and, of course, pornography.

                    ENOCH (CONT'D)
          When can you have it by? Today?

                    TALIB
          I still gotta go to work. I'll try to get
          the pens for you tomorrow.

                    ENOCH
          Your brother would get it today. I wish he
          was here. Where is he anyway?

                    TALIB
          Farid's still in rehab, Dad. I'm sure he
          would help if he could.

ENOCH

That fucking alcohol got a hold of him. I
wish he would just stop drinking.

TALIB

I know, we all do.

ENOCH
(prideful)
He's just like his old man. I used to be the
same way. Maaaaaaan, I was a summamabitch.
Everyone in my infantry told me I woulda
been a war criminal if I went to Vietnam. I
was baaaad. They hated me. *Hahaha! Whooo!*

TALIB

...I know. Can I get you anything else?

ENOCH

I'll take some orange juice.

TALIB

All right.

Talib goes out to the kitchen and pours his father a
glass of juice. He breaks the fourth wall once again.

TALIB (CONT'D)
I'm not claiming to be in a great place
about all this or anything, but I know
hardcore helped me through all his
bullshit growing up. Hearing someone
scream "Rise above" or "You can't change
the world, but you can change yourself"

as a kid and knowing that they're
talking directly to you is pretty fucking
empowering. I believed it. I didn't fit
into the norms of my surroundings and
hardcore was like, "Fuck them all, society
is shit, I'm not gonna let them get me."
That meant everything to me.

He heads back in the room and hands his father
the glass.

                    ENOCH
          Thank you, Talib.

                    TALIB
          No problem. I'm gonna go kick it with Mom
          for a minute.

As Talib is about to walk out of the room, his
father says—

                    ENOCH
          Talib, I know I'm difficult. I know I
          wasn't always there for you, but if you
          could, I'd really appreciate it if you'd—

Talib talks to the camera in anticipation.

                    TALIB (TO CAMERA)
          Holy shit, is this it? Is this the moment
          I've been waiting for? Is he going to

                                        (MORE)

finally own up to all the bullshit and
attitude about who I am and ask me for an
apolog—

                    ENOCH
—get me a nasty magazine. Please? I need
it. Something really dirty, okay?

Talib nods his head at his father and quietly
leaves the room.

                    TALIB
              (chuckling to camera)
Long story short, I ain't changing him
and I don't want to. I didn't change who I
was for him either, and that was cause I
had an anthem and a community. That's what
hardcore was and is for me, just what I
needed, right when I needed it. I was born
a punk and I'm—

From beyond the door, Enoch yells out—

                    ENOCH
     TAAAAAALLLLLIIB!

Talib gives us an annoyed look.

                    TALIB
I'm... (deep sigh) I'm not buying him a
fucking porno magazine.

Talib goes back in the room.

                                        END.

NO FUN: BE CAREFUL WHAT YOU ASK FOR . . . DAD

COMIC

JAMES SPOONER

"In many ways punk and hard-core raised me. Where the community failed me, I've taken it upon myself to clean up the mess for the next generation."

MUSIC MEANS FREE

NONFICTION

COURTNEY LONG

"Whether by the sound of fierce joy, screeching rage, or heart-aching croons, Black punks take and create a space for themselves and the shared Black experience."

HAVE YOU EVER FELT STICKY ON THE INSIDES? I MEAN THE VERY insides. Where the throat is a garden hose that flows to a stomach like a dirty old purse.

Not a new garden hose, one of those old ones where the water pressure is off. Sticky like that, where the sides are touching each other and you can't figure out where the knot is, and there must be a knot somewhere for the insides to be touching like that.

You can see the hole where the mouth starts, the tiny teeth and the swollen tongue. The knot can't be there. So, you go searching for it where it all ends—at the bottom of the old dirty purse. I mean the kind of purse your grandma tried to give you from the back of her closet. Where it's chunky and bulky and smells of mothballs and you can't find anything but old crumbs.

I feel sticky like that sometimes (all the time). So sticky. When I try to scream sometimes (all the time), it feels like sound is caught behind the knot and sputtering; caught behind the knot and boiling up in an old purse that was never meant to hold anything.

That's what it felt like when I got the call, and back then I always used to get the calls. I always used to go to the hospital. I always used to try to scream sound and would only throw up crumbs.

That's what music means to me.

So when I got the call (I always got the calls), I smelled the collar before I put it on. It smelled of sweat—yours and mine. It smelled of dark basements, cheap beer, and one-dollar waters. I always bought them too big. To this day, they are still too big. For a moment, I swam in the long sleeves, lost in the darkness of cool cotton. Then, it hits just past my hip in that awkward sweet spot between shirt and dress. I hide my thumbs in the excess fabric; I hide my breasts and my ass. Here I am genderless. Here I am cold. Here I am nobody against the press of bodies and under the shadows of sound.

At the hospital, however, I am his daughter. Shirt or no shirt.

The whole establishment smells of hand sanitizer and Lysol wipes. The smell wafts off everything I touch. I don't like it. I curl my fingers in the too-long sleeves and make them mittens. I punch elevator buttons and hold railings this way. I clutch counters and ask for directions; ask for name tags; ask for the bathroom and promptly walk back out. I feel cold and sticky in the constant artificial breeze. The lights are sharp and clinical. I'm nervous that even under the mysterious mustard stain on my chest, everyone I pass can see the dark outline of my bra; I'm nervous that my sneakers smell like the liquor I'd been standing in, and squelch down the hallway; I'm nervous when I find the doors; I'm nervous when I stand outside them.

"Taking Back Sunday? I love that band."

I turn like they called my name. His face is faceless here in this place, but the smile is genuine and he is pointing at me. The garden hose, knot undone. The words come easy. "They are my favorite; I love them too."

"I think they had a show a week ago, right? So awesome they come through Detroit."

"Right! Played the whole album back to front."

"Takes me back to high school!" He chuckles and waves, headed back the way I came. Away.

I open the door. For a moment not thinking. Without mittens. Not squelching, just stepping in.

Smiling.

He's in a blue gown with snaps this time, not white with twill tape ties. The whole family knows he showed up in a suit. Was it blue? Or just the tie and pocket square? He always shows up in a suit. He thinks it will guarantee him better service and stop racism in its tracks. I hug him and he feels small. His legs look spindly. It feels like every week he loses more weight. I tease him about his open-back gown and shake his arm up and down playfully. The medical bracelet has replaced his gold watch. It doesn't make the jingle I was used to, it's a new *swish-swish* barely there, a sound that I am now getting used to. He is grumpy and happy at the same time.

"You didn't need to do this," he reminds me, but I did. I always get the call. He sits half on and half off the bed, as if this will help make him not a patient. He has stretched the tubes as far from him as they will go. I flutter around him and his collection of poles and dripping bags, as if not sitting will not make him a patient. I tease him for watching football like we are in his living room, and his collection of poles and dripping bags are just the side tables around his leather recliner. My hand gets caught in a tube and we both act like it didn't happen. When the door snaps open, we are both startled.

"Blood draw," the nurse calls out, towing a cart. It is a man with hair in his eyes and arms strong with experience. Here in this place, his face is faceless. He whips the cart around expertly with barely a wheel squeak.

It makes him sigh and the garden hose knot. There is a brown couch in his room—I sit, and it crinkles underneath me like tissue paper. He doesn't say anything when the nurse lifts his arm, just sighs again. His wrists act like they don't care to have hands. Under the lights, he is pale and yellow. Under the lights, I can suspect his white great-grandfather. Under the lights, he looks tired, like the word has been carved into his bones.

The garden hose knots, and my ankles cross with the feeling. When you have sticky insides, you start to feel the stickiness everywhere—as if you are so sticky you will adhere to everything; my ankles to each other; butt to the couch; ears to my shoulders; hands to my elbows. All sticky as insides touch insides and wrench back and forth. The pressure builds even here; beneath the constant artificial breeze you are hot, hot, hot.

The blood is red and ruby at the same time. The nurse is an expert, so his eyes wander, from the needle and the rapidly filling vial to his grumpy patient who pretends to be focused on a game on TV that he doesn't know how to play, and land curiously on me. He meant to look away, a slow scan of his surroundings. But I am sticky, so his eyes got stuck.

I didn't know I was crying until his eyes got stuck.

"You have a strong father!" The nurse practically shouts with an encouraging fist pump. He gestures at the blood like it's proof.

My father's head jerks around, instantly irritated, first at the nurse who isn't even looking at him, and then to see what the nurse is looking at. He jerks again in surprise, and the nurse must steady the needle.

He has learned to spurt blood with minimal prompting, and I have learned to spurt tears without moving a single muscle.

"Really?!" My father is shouting now too. "It's just a blood draw, every few hours, nothing's wrong!"

I turn my whole body away in one movement, and the couch practically snarls. My stomach is an old purse—you can't find nothing but crumbs in its chunky, bulky pockets.

I don't want to show the crumbs.

I don't want to show the crumbs.

I don't want to show the crumbs, but there is a knot in the garden hose and the water pressure is off.

I pull my shirt up over my eyes like I'm four again and not twenty-four. It smells of sweat—yours and mine. It smelled of dark basements, cheap beer, and one-dollar waters. For a moment, I swim, lost in the darkness of cool cotton in the excess fabric. Here I am genderless. Here I am cold. Here I am nobody against the press of bodies and under the shadows of sound.

My father is still shouting, then cajoling, now speaking conversationally with the nurse. Now they are friends. Now they are laughing. I know without looking that they show each other the full ruby vials and declare them nothing. "This is nothing!" he says again and again. Along with "This is just monitoring," and "how can you go back to school to be a doctor if you can't handle this?"

I don't remind him I don't want to be a doctor. I don't turn around until the door snaps closed; until the crumbles have crawled back into the old purse, though the taste of them still lingers. My father jiggles the tubes and bags and poles like they are just tubes and bags and poles. Until the liquids slosh around. He picks at his gown like it is something he threw on. "Why would you get upset when I am in the safest place I can be?"

His voice is stern when he calls me over. "That's like yelling fire in a firehouse." He takes my hands with firm grips and firm wrists, then shoves tissues at me and grumbles about the score on the TV. He is grumpy and happy simultaneously when I leave him. Half in and half out of the bed.

It takes me a long time to start the car. For a while I just stare out the windshield at cement blocks. For a while I just focus on my breath whistling in and out past the taste of crumbs, the knots, the churning in my belly. Then I turn the key.

The guitar sneaks in first, riffs scratchy and melodic, and the hair rises on my arms. Then the drums enter stage right, slow, steady, and familiar. I put my foot on the gas pedal. As soon as the clean vocals have started, I am leaning on the drumbeats and turning the steering wheel. I wonder if the band knew that those beginning notes sounded like pulsing atriums and ventricles. I wonder if the band knew that the song, where they sounded like they were having the most fun, would catapult them into the galaxies of stardom. By the time the drumbeats are mimicking arrhythmias and the vocals are busy blurring the lines between singing and screaming, my windows are down. I'm leaving behind the smells of hand sanitizer and Lysol wipes with every mile; running away from trailing tubes and ruby vials. I'm screaming at the top of my lungs, remembering the clashing lights, the press of bodies, the moshing. For once, I'm screaming at the top of my lungs and not caring who hears me. In those moments, nothing can knot me. There is no space for crumbs when sound is all-encompassing. Sound is everything. Sound vibrates eardrums. Sound is louder than heavy breathing. Louder than heartbeats, louder than thinking.

That's what music means to me.

STANDING ON THE VERGE

NONFICTION

HANIF ABDURRAQIB

"The first punk
show I went to
was Chemo Kids
in Cincinnati,
back in 2001."

DON'T KNOW WHAT CORNER OF MYTHOLOGY IT COMES FROM, BUT I have always been fascinated by this idea that performing through extreme, infinite grief is a sign of toughness or triumph. I suppose it maybe begins with obsessing over that which can be conquered. Even greater if that which can be conquered is massive, but unseen. I wasn't on anyone's clock but my own the summer my mother crossed over from the touchable world to whatever comes after it, but I didn't wanna do shit except stay in my room in the ways not all that different from how they'd always been: me fucking around on a stereo, recording the occasional tune off of the radio, losing myself in early teenage anxieties while the long days flickered out. That was my excuse, though. Even in my younger years, I was always living in preparation for grief.

There's something about punk that has always opened itself up to my understanding about living through and performing through grief's long shadow. It could be because me and all of my pals ran toward shows and each other to escape the immense sadnesses of our shared or disparate lives, and it could be because so many of the songs I loved were about thrashing up against something immovable—be it emotional or political—which seemed to fit the bill of what I thought grief to be. But it was also, I think, because I fell into punk first because I was fighting to be understood, frustrated by the world that didn't seem to want to understand me. That was one of the first wounds I carried, and punk was one of the first places that I felt that wound tended to.

Because America is a country with an insatiable appetite for both competition and proof, there is much to be made of a scene where an athlete plays through physical pain—the visuals and dramatics of it all. It's not unlike the fervor that is whipped up when an athlete plays through emotional anguish, something that many people can only imagine but not entirely access. I will get to the tunes and What It All Means in a moment, but indulge my spiral into the tale of Isiah Thomas and Isaiah Thomas. Both undersized guards, probably too small for the league but too tough to take anyone's shit, and so they weren't really all that small because when you grow up on courts and in hoods where you're the smallest kid around, you learn a thing or two about how to survive, what will or will not kill you. And in the 1988 NBA finals, the Bad Boys from Detroit were finna take down those flashy Showtime motherfuckers from LA, or at least that was the plan before their star point guard, Isiah Thomas, rolled his ankle something real bad, writhing on the ground in the kinda way that anyone who watches enough ball knows isn't a performance. He'd scored fourteen points in the third quarter before that ankle went out on him. He left the game, came back, and dropped eleven more points on one leg to get the Pistons a two-point lead. Thomas finished with forty-three points, but the Lakers lost on a bad call from the ref and that's the way it goes. Series went to a game seven, and Thomas could barely play. He went back out on one leg because he knew it had to be then or not at all. There's a cost.

In April of 2017, Isaiah Thomas's sister was killed in a car crash the day before his Boston Celtics were set to take on the Chicago Bulls in game one of the playoffs. Thomas, stricken by grief, decided he'd still play in the game. He put up thirty-three points and dragged the Celtics as far as he could, before they faltered, losing by six. The Celtics eventually won the series and went far in the playoffs, before Thomas was taken out by a hip injury—an injury that cost him a chance at a large payday that would have been on the way if he'd have just stayed healthy through the playoff run. But still, America marveled at his resilience, and they still do, even as he bounces around from NBA team to NBA team, a fraction of what he was.

All this probably seems like it has little to do with the fact that I don't know much about Eddie Hazel's mother. Certainly not as much as I want to. If you are a true Funkadelic head, you might know the name Grace Cook, even if you don't know that Grace Cook is the mother of Eddie Hazel. The 1974 Funkadelic album *Standing on the Verge of Getting It On* marked Hazel's return into the arms of the mothership after departing following *Maggot Brain* in 1971. In the liner notes of the album, almost every contribution by Hazel, both songwriting and guitar playing, was credited to Grace Cook. On the '75 release *Let's Take It to the Stage*, Hazel is credited on only the first two songs, just as "G. Cook." This, it seems, was about contractual issues and publishing rights. But also, by that point, Hazel had effectively been replaced in the band after charges for assault and drug possession landed him in jail. While he was there, George Clinton heard some young hotshot guitarist from Ohio named Michael Hampton playing a cover of Hazel's "Maggot Brain," note for note at a party, and just like that, Hampton was filling the Hazel-shaped void within the Mothership.

Hazel's return to the group was sometimes fraught with the tension between who he was to the band and who he was still fighting to become. A strange wind blows you away, and things ain't the same when you get blown back.

I don't know as much as I wish I knew about Grace Cook except that in '67, George Clinton showed up at her house and begged Grace Cook to let her seventeen-year-old son play some songs with him and his band. Cook, who had moved her whole family to Plainfield, New Jersey, from Brooklyn to keep her kids safe from drugs and crime, handed her baby over to the ever-expanding universe of George Clinton and all the delights and devils it held.

The story that you've probably heard goes something like this: George Clinton was in the studio during the recording session, floating off LSD, and he looks over to Eddie Hazel before the recording starts and tells him to play the guitar in his hands as if his mother had just died.

That's an abbreviated version of the fuller Clinton quote, and I suppose it might not make too much of a difference to anyone who hasn't lost a mother, or a father, or a person who has cradled them in a moment of spiraling anguish. But the full quote is: "I told him to play like his mother had died, to picture that day, what he would feel, how he would make sense of his life, how he would take a measure of everything that was inside him."

This latter part explains what happens on "Maggot Brain" more than anything else, to me. It isn't just the death, but also the reckoning. It's also the wandering, meandering emptiness and small explosions that exist within it. The parts of Hazel's playing that I admire the most on "Maggot Brain" come when the fluidity is disrupted, when the guitar stutters, begins to flow again and then stops, begins and then stops, before giving in to a torrential wave of sound. This is the sound of how one makes sense of their life after becoming unmoored, drifting in the hell of fresh grief. Running up against a wall repeatedly, until some cracks begin to show through.

"Maggot Brain" was recorded in one take. Every other musician on the track was largely faded out by Clinton in the mix, so that Hazel could be the highlight. Also in the mix, there were delays added, to offer a kind of echoing effect, Hazel's guitar echoing back on itself multiple times, to create a sort of eeriness, a haunting of sound.

For a long time in my life, I was the writer that people ran to in the immediate moments after someone beloved passed away. I was known as the person capable of writing a quick obituary for anyone with a wide, immersive life. This, I would explain, is because I believe that if you love anyone enough—through their work or their real, touchable life—then you have already mourned the world without them in it. But to put it more simply: if you are someone for whom every loss feels like a small apocalypse, it behooves you to prepare for the ending of another world by imagining how you might navigate it.

This, in part, is why I have always been obsessed with the full Clinton ask. Hazel's mother was still alive, and just as I don't know much about Grace Cook, I cannot speculate on how much Eddie Hazel loved her. I can assume she loved him a good deal. At least enough to want to hold him close, to free him from the sounds of gunfire at night. I know that kind of love well enough to say that it is real. And here, at twenty-one, Hazel was being asked to imagine stepping into a world without whatever love there was between them.

Some songs are long because it feels like the architect of the songs doesn't want them to end. Like maybe they know that they've captured some singular magic and that nothing on the other side of that will ever be the same. Though I have done it here, against my desires and instincts, I don't like to romanticize the heights that death (or even the imagination of it) can carry one to. It isn't that Hazel didn't find himself in the throes of the occasional miracle after "Maggot Brain," it is that the song itself is a song that anyone who puts hands on any instrument in the name of seeking out a single sound would kill to have as their own. It's an entire prayer service—the whisper and the wail. An unfurling of microscopic conversations between one person, one instrument, one deep well of imagination.

Across a bar one night some years ago, someone yelled at one of my pals who tossed "Maggot Brain" on the juke, and I suppose the yelling stranger had a point. When the quarters are lined up, and everyone is eager to get their time, it is probably uncharitable to find a ten-minute song and let it rip as one of your picks, especially a ten-minute song as thick to wade through as this one. It also bears mentioning that this incident unfolded in a punk bar, which is of consequence, because most of the songs rattling out of the juke that night were of the short, fast, and loud variety. And here we were, slogging through an epic of a dirge with few discernable words.

The debate of what does or doesn't make one "punk" is the least interesting debate that can be had. It flattens the wide range of experiences and containers that many of us—especially any of us at the margins—came into punk, what we got out of it, and how it defined our lives beyond records. To ascribe some binary to it based off of sound or aesthetics fails the vast imagination of what punk is, what it has done, and what it can do for people first stumbling into it, and how it can still evolve for those of us who have been immersed in it for years. But in the case of Hazel, this debate rises up most usefully when considering fame versus infamy. How dangerous one's legacy is versus how dangerous they actually were. How quickly they maybe burned out to those only familiar with their brightest moment.

I once paid too much damn money for Eddie Hazel's 1977 solo record *Games, Dames, and Guitar Thangs* mostly because I had to have it and there weren't too many copies of it around. The album fell out of print shortly after it went into circulation. Still, to this day, a good-condition copy might run you a few hundred in the right place (or the wrong place). The album itself isn't memorable outside of Hazel's flip of both "California Dreamin'" and "I Want You (She's So Heavy)," but it is sort of a perfect time capsule of Hazel, then six years removed from his greatest moment, not even attempting to chase it, the way some might after seeing the top of some rare mountain. By that point, he'd served his prison time, he'd left Funkadelic and come back, he'd worked on Motown with the Temptations, among others. The argument I made once, in regards to Hazel's so-called punk chops, is that all the punks I knew and loved the most knew when they couldn't chase an older, maybe greater version of themselves anymore, and they had to give in to whatever subdued but potentially still great version of themselves there still was. I am sorry to return to sports once again, but to see Isaiah Thomas, who played himself through grief and injury, trying to chase the greatest era he's ever had while his body simply won't allow for it, is somewhat heartbreaking. To know thyself is punk, and to accept what comes with the passage of time is punk. Strummer knew this, and I suppose so did Lydon, though I'd argue that the Pistols were never as great as what came after them for him. But both Strummer and Lydon's second (and third, and beyond) acts illuminated what I came to love most about punk: so many of the punks I knew or admired growing up were starting from what many would consider a bare-bones aesthetic. Understanding themselves mostly in relation to ease—even the most serious musicians who dipped into punk were doing it with a minimalist approach. What this does for many folks is allows reinvention to arrive easy. You're not a blank slate, by any means. But you're a malleable one. I was drawn to punk by the unexpected, and when the unexpected is on the table, transformation is endlessly possible.

Hazel knew this, too. There were those who saw Hazel play late in his life, with some stitched-together version of P-Funk All-Stars, where he faded into the background, and quietly played only the notes required to move the song forward. His playing, as skilled as it still was, became an act of service, and less of a showcase, as it might have been in 1971, in a studio where he closed his eyes, imagined a funeral, and pressed his hands to the strings.

When I was first learning what poems were and how to write them, I came across the Adrian Matejka poem "Maggot Brain" from his book *Mixology*. It was one of the first poems I'd read that made me feel like I could write poems the way I wanted to. It was distinctly about a musician—dedicated to Eddie Hazel—but it held so much more beyond that. The line that echoed for days, weeks, and months after reading it was this one, which comes near the poem's ending: "maggot brain, somebody somewhere is losing a mama right now."

The morning my mother died, the only lasting memory I have is of my grandmother, my father's mother. She was upstairs, loudly sobbing, shouting why not me. Why couldn't it have been me. I believe this memory hovers for me now because it is the thing that reminds me how arbitrary loss is, and therefore how simple it is to completely imagine anyone being gone at any moment. My grandmother, a

woman then in her seventies who took down multiple packs of cigarettes per day, in absolute awe at the possibility that she outlived
a woman decades younger than she was, praying for an impossible
exchange of lives.

The point I believed Matejka was getting at was bending toward this
inevitability that I find myself cherishing, particularly as I both age
and continue to create things as I do so. There is no guarantee that
any of us will stumble upon a golden moment, and there is no guarantee that whatever carries us there will linger long enough to be
accessed again. There is another, less cynical way to interpret what
Matejka was saying, this idea that if there is loss everywhere, there
is something to rise to the occasion for. But I make better use of the
phrase with my understanding: loss is arbitrary and at times un-
spectacular. A powerful temporary vessel, but not a permanent one.
It can unlock the magic, but then the key is hard to find after the
unlocking.

Eddie Hazel died in 1992 at only forty-two years old. I have spent
time trying to find out if his mother died before he did, but have
had no luck, since so little of her life exists on the internet. But I
can't shake the thought of Grace Cook having to bury her son, while
still alive herself, despite being once imagined dead. "Maggot Brain"
was played at Hazel's funeral, of course. Which leads me to consider
what it is to have outlived the worst corner of someone's imagination. To know that there was a wailing once, and it was for you.

DREAD[S]

FICTION

MARCUS CLAYTON

"Check out punk's ethos, not just the sound, and you'll find Black punk everywhere. Black artists are able to express themselves without the constraint of whiteness."

PUNKS DO NOT GIVE A SHIT ABOUT US. THEY ARE SCOWLING STATues, at best tolerating the space we take from them. We set up our equipment for a gig at a run-down pizza parlor in Bend, Oregon. Our first show outside of Southern California and our own punk circles. The scowls know who we are, though; our name seared into their local flyers—multicolored papers decomposing in gutters like the autumn leaves we stepped on to get inside the venue. We are Pipebomb!, with exclamation point always accompanying the letters.

On drums, Id y Yacht, real name [Redacted—all you need to know about us are our chosen punk names]. Our token white ally, our beast. His blast beats create quakes to shatter dance floors and force feet to move. Look at his clothes: Richard Spencer haircut to trick white punks into safety, checkered dress shirt and khakis straight from work, suede boots with laces he bought from a yard sale at Exene Cervenka's home.

On bass and vox, [Redacted—his identity is his own to share, to keep, to want], better known to us as Upper Duck. He plays ducttaped instruments, wears a black Cannibal Corpse T-shirt, wears a Mexican mustache gifted from his father's genes, wears jet-black hair molded by Suavecito Pomade. Duck knows little of his father's language, and his skin is glossed like his ancestors' Spanish colonizers, but he will scream Chicano before wearing an American flag.

On guitar and other vox, [I do not wear the name picked by Mamá and Pops. How I wish to tell them the name is not in a garbage bin, but a closet with a nice wooden hanger. For now.] Blacky Moose. These days, only Moose. I am covered in roses, designs stitched into a white short-sleeve button-up, tucked into torn black jeans covering filthy black and white Chucks. A beard shields my face, tattoos coat the high yellow on my right arm [I swear it is not shame when each parent wanted a child a shade Browner or a shade Blacker and had to compromise], and dark brown dreadlocks cage my eyes from direct contact with white punks; [most effective months from now. Pipebomb! plays a show in Anaheim, California, southeast of our hometowns in Southeast LA. Los Angeles punks know of us, or at least know the exclamation point is part of the aesthetic. Some know our punk names, but remain unaware that I dropped "Blacky" before the Bend show.

"You're Blacky, right?" a drunk man asks at the Anaheim show.

"Just Moose," I say.

"Oh, okay," he relents. "Is that an Indian flag?"

Over my amplifier, I hang a Costa Rican flag. Being mixed, strangers make a game out of guessing my ethnicities. You're Black and something else, which is true. Sometimes people know my other half is Latino. Other times, I get something like Croatian, or Hawaiian, or half white—the latter of which physically hurts me, so the flag helps me avoid the pain.

"It's the Costa Rican flag," I say, proud.

"Oh, you like Costa Rica?" a drunk man asks at the Anaheim show.

"I'm half Costa Rican."

"I see," he says. "You know, I've been to Belize."

"Tight," I lie.

After the show, we wheel our equipment past white punks who say things like, *They're not really punk. Songs about Black or Brown power or whatever shit? Thinkin' they're MLK or some bullshit? Nah. They slow down too much, pretendin' to be Fugazi. Thinkin' too hard instead of just lettin' loose and breaking shit. Motherfucker was wearing flowers on his shirt, for Christ's sake. They ain't gritty like Agnostic Front or Minor Threat. You can't convince me that band knows anything about the streets.* My dreadlocks save me, fallen over my eyes to stop me from placing a face to the words. I do not see all the punks huddled around curbsides and streetlights smoking cigarettes and using their phones. All of them white. Duck and I transform into splotches. I do not see Yacht's mouth when he screams POSERS! at the crowd who did not care for us. As I pack my equipment into the van, I do not see Yacht come face-to-face with a white punk bedazzled in metal studs and FEAR patches, bright red mohawk stretching into the sky like war missiles. Though I hear the words, I just don't care about spic and nigger songs, bro, and I hear the crash of bone on teeth and bedazzled studs collide with the ground. The noise reverberates within the cavern of my hair. I do not see Duck pull Yacht away, say, Fuck these foos. We got better shows coming up, anyway. I see nothing.

But, right now,] my dreadlocks shelter my eyes from about a hundred punks standing in the pizza parlor. This is the largest audience we've ever had. All the white punks wear the costumes: studded leather everything, multicolored mohawks, black shit-kickers galore, and needle-point tattoos inked by jittery friends. Many of them coked out of their minds; a blonde girl wearing a GBH shirt twirls around in the pit before we play any songs, her eyes dilated enough for me to see among the clustered front line of crusted clothes and rainbowed spikes attached to pasty white boys. There are Brown and Black punks in here, sure. They line the back of the parlor; wallflowers kicked out of the center by the violent typhoons of white slamdancers.

Every scowl in front of us has skin the shade of chalk, and stands arms crossed in defiance of our existence, [which is the default mood in venues back home in Los Angeles, of course. Our hometown houses shows that ask Pipebomb! to play at the last possible minute, preying on our desperation to stretch our legs, praying Duck and I stand in front to show promoters' diversity. These are the shows that tuck us away at the 1 a.m. slots of a five-band show—a packed house from 9 p.m. to 11:30 p.m., but folks get tired after midnight, so we play to a promoter and a couple of unlucky friends]. In front of us stands a bald, white punk with a ragged "GOD SAVE THE QUEEN" Sex Pistols shirt—the shirt itself an off-white with a Union Jack splayed under the images. His crossed arms covered in more tattoos than mine, though faded and gray from age.

He yells, "I thought this was a punk show? What's with the flowers?" as though the tight torn leather pants squeezed the words out of his torso, not a single syllable in a British accent like his shirt promised. We ignore the white punk and play. We never start with "1, 2, 3, 4s" like the Ramones would have you believe. Yacht hits his snare once before belting out blast beats like bullets, then Duck's bass rumbles tremors into the linoleum of the parlor as my guitar fuzz becomes furious ocean waves crashing into walls. Now, the flowers on my buttoned shirt are ferocious.

People react to us, for better and worse.

Mosh pits flare for the rest our set; the Black and Brown kids even feel safe to unglue themselves from the walls. In the cacophony, some hop off tables. Others climb over my amplifier to jump into the crowd. This is the energy we live for—back home, movement is mandatory, marginalized punks releasing demons gifted from oppression in the dance circles, finding each other's rhythm to bare unity believed to be fables. When songs end, some scream, "More!" Others scream, "Fuck me up!" to fill the silence between songs their cocaine brains cannot stand. None of this is the polite applause of empty bars. This is the earthquake that shatters buildings built by old money, the masters' tools smelted into a language we use to speak over white words. For thirty minutes, we are the loudest band on the planet.

Adrenaline keeps my body warm after the set in twenty-degree weather. Sweat soaked through clothes, but we load equipment back into the rental van while accepting hugs from punks who stopped us to say they loved our set. Two Black punks are especially glowing from the show, sweat glistening through their pink G.L.O.S.S. and white Death Grips shirts. We swap moisture through embrace, and they go on about how great it was to see an old Black punk in their scene. I am twenty-seven, I am high yellow.

"Old?" I ask, nearly saying, "Black?" [but, luckily, I have learned better to not talk, not to complicate the community with whatever grad school bullshit fed into me from white dudes. My tongue slipped once, and recently—a backyard show with four bands of color, donations to accrue bail funds for friends, DIY merch made on the spot by QTPOC punks. One band had a mindful Black singer who started one song with "this shit is for all my fellow colored people who are targeted by pigs every fuckin' day," which got positive cheers by everyone but me.

"Why is it problematic?" Black punk will ask after his set, when all my praise for his music gets extinguished when I point out his banter.

"Because 'colored people' is antiquated and offensive, especially toward Black people."

"My dad says 'colored people' all the time. He's Black. He's been through some white shenanigans, too. How can he be offensive toward Black people?"

"I'm not saying your dad is offensive, it's just not a widely accepted term."

"Okay, then what the fuck do we gotta say?"

"People of color."

"That's the same thing."

"It's actually quite different."

"You throw in the word *of* and it makes *colored people* sound less like *nigger*? Who makes these rules?"

"Look—trust me: the phrase *people of color* is doing work. Saying *colored people* is just too close to the n-word."

"But why is *colored people* bad when *people of color* literally uses the same words? Doesn't that make *people of color* just as bad?"

"Because . . . because . . . because . . ."]

So, I take the praise and smile quietly so that the Black punks can hold their joy as they walk back into the pizza parlor. We finish loading our things, readying ourselves to see the next band. I had tied my dreadlocks into a ponytail to better see where to go despite the warmth they could offer from the cold. For once, I wanted to see faces, and I wanted mine to catch the frost from the Oregon cold—arrogance, I guess, knowing the adrenaline hugging my veins meant the frost would fail. Even though the chill staves off our bodies, I know this won't last long, so I find a sweater. I hold it in my hands as we close the van doors. Still, I am warm. Between the punks of color and seeing all the white punks bow to our music, I am frightened by the genuine smile baked by the warmth.

"Hot damn! That half-nigger can shred!" the bald, white punk says with an entire chest. He is by the entrance door, washed into a group of punks who "nervous laugh" his words away. [If you are Black—even, or especially, partially Black—or any ~~colored person~~ person of color, you will pause. In the air of this pause is the disbelief that what you heard is what you heard. The dull, naïve voice in your head will shriek, "It is (insert any year after 1865), this can't still be happening!" Once that voice quiets, the reminders wash back in: don't wear your hair too nappy or dreaded in a nice restaurant unless you want patrons staring at you the entire meal, don't listen to rap music with the windows down unless you want people to think you're ghetto, don't bash your light skin if you have it because it keeps you from being called a "full" nigger like your real Black relatives.

If you are not Black or any ~~colored person~~ person of color, you'll want to be the hero; the ally pulling oppressed bodies out of fires. Look at the white punk with disgust and shake your head. Or, film the white punk, post it somewhere on social media, hope strangers see it and make it viral, hope their vitriol gets the white punk fired from his job if he has a job. Or, tell a booker, or his daytime employee or manager. Or,] Yacht rushes the white punk; I see his hand struggle to not become a fist, to not make the punk's eye as black as the wallflowers. Yacht vomits other profanities to become louder than slurs—let the punk know his language is not welcomed. The other white punks look on in confusion, the wallflowers look with optimistic fear. For a moment, the parking lot is completely quiet, the white punk's mouth agape, holds his hands out like he's had enough—no defeat, only annoyance. Says, "Okay! Okay!" while waving goodbye. Duck and I watch, frozen along the walls of the van, my dreadlocks tied to watch the whole scene. My muscles tell me to tag in, let Yacht's voice take a rest, but Duck simply says, "Fuck that foo," alluding to the fact that we'll have "Better shows after this," as though holding me back from a fight I cannot win [because this is Yacht's victory. A real punk motherfucker. Watch his cape flap in the Podunk Oregon wind. Now look around; see everyone where they were before the fight. See nothing change. No applause for sticking up for ~~Black people~~ ~~people of color~~ colored people in absentia.

Now see Yacht inert, maybe coming to, maybe waiting for approval—a real punk motherfucker who wants to give a shit,] but then a friend of Yacht, a different white punk who got us this gig, swears it was a compliment. *Nigger* is a good word, Yacht's friend argues. Like Patti Smith said. The two exchange more words, but one verbal arm twist later, Yacht's friend tells the white punk it was "not cool" to say that. "Not cool." Imagine a racial slur being put on the same pedestal as out-of-season shoes.

Suddenly, it is cold again.

Inside, I stand at the back of the parlor with the other Brown and Black punks, telling myself it is solidarity. Duck joins Yacht in the mosh pits for the next band, deciding against standing with me and the other colored wallflowers. My arms are crossed in LA contempt as I observe with the fellow wallflowers. The last band is all white and play traditional hardcore, all of them wearing the same studded leather clothing as everyone else. The reaction they receive is bigger than ours. Relentless mosh pits swinging fists and boots. Some grab the singer's microphone to scream out-of-sync gibberish. A chair catches fire from a purposeful Bic lighter, then punks leap over the flame like a ritual. At the end, the band wrecks their equipment: guitar necks snapped against amplifiers, cymbals slash snare heads. The bassist throws his instrument in the air, knocking loose a piece of ceiling that collides with another punk's head. The bass itself cracks the ground, the punk's head bleeds to the rhythm of cheers and cheers and cheers.

The wallflowers say nothing, voices trapped in the maelstrom of white chaos, even their hands go mute when it is time for applause. My hands crawl to the top of my head to undo the locks; they fall over my face like prison cell bars, but then cloud the cheers from my ears as though the sun was being hidden from the earth. This is how we live, anyway—within static where our voices should be so clear, but white noise consumes all the good sound.

They pretend to care about us[, then pretend to be us].

THE PROGENITORS OF BLACK FEMINIST PUNK:
SISTA GRRRL RIOT

NONFICTION

LAINA DAWES

"I felt that the history of Sista Grrrl Riot should be properly documented by the founders of these groundbreaking events."

The flyer for the first Sista Grrrl Riot, 1998. Provided by Honeychild Coleman.

STARTING ON VALENTINE'S DAY, 1998, NEW YORK CITY–BASED MUsicians Honeychild Coleman, Tamar-Kali Brown, Simantha M. Sernaker (a.k.a. Simi Stone), and Maya Sokora produced a series of concerts under the moniker Sista Grrrl Riot. Using their connections to New York's indie music venues, they took turns producing shows, creating flyers, and arranging each evening's festivities, resulting in an "Afropunk" space before Afro-Punk existed.

Since there is a desire to mythologize the past to make sense of the future, there have been rumors and innuendos over the years regarding what Sista Grrrl Riot was about. To be honest, nothing has come close to the magic this collective produced since then, as the amount of Manhattan-based live music venues has shrunk, and those that survived through the 2008 economic collapse, gentrification, and the COVID-19 pandemic are not as socially, culturally, and racially diverse as they should be in a bustling, cosmopolitan city. So, while all the women have gone on to advance their solo careers, they agreed to sit down for a group chat to talk about what it was like being young, Black, and ambitious creatives who carved out a space to define themselves and their music on their own terms.

How did you meet?

Honey C: I want to say we met in '96. A friend had met and invited Tamar-Kali over for dinner. We saw you walk in and we're like, "Yo, there's a really cool woman in here. Let's go steal her out of the kitchen." And I remember thinking, "Damn, she's cool."

Simi: When I met Honeychild, I thought she was the coolest chick I'd ever seen. I think she rolled up on a skateboard with a guitar.

Honey C: When I met Simi, she had a pack of cigarettes in the strap of her bra, a black lace bra on and boxer shorts rolled up like hot pants, with a violin. I happened to be playing a gig at Brownies [a former rock club in downtown Manhattan], and Simi was one or two acts before me, and I was transfixed, and I was like, "Who is this girl, breaking my heart with the fricking violin?" I had previously met Maya through my brother [collaborator], Jerome, who played with me, and he was telling me all about her. When I first saw her play live, I rushed the stage like a maniac to get to her.

Maya: Right, right. Yeah. And so, they've been telling me about you [Tamar-Kali]. And then there was that show at Acme Underground. As part of my set, I did a cover of a Betty Davis song. I remember knowing that you were there and feeling like, "Okay, this is cool," because I was part of a rock scene. I knew these Black guys in a band, and they had told me about you. When I knew that you were there that night, I had to kind of shut it out because I was a little intimidated. Seriously. I was like, "Here's this other Black rock woman that I've been hearing about who is so powerful." And I could feel you were there. Like, I could feel it. It was like, shit. All right. Fine. And then when the lights are in your face and stuff starts going on, you forget everything. And then I started into the Betty Davis song, and you came up in front of the stage. You rushed the stage.

Tamar-Kali: And I watched the stage like she owed me money, like I was on stage. I was like, "Oh . . ."

Maya: Really, you know? And you did. You looked angry. And then I remember after the show, you were threatening to beat my ass . . .

Tamar-Kali: Because you did the damn thing. That's how we do.

Maya: That was your introduction to me. I know. I was like, okay, how fucked up is this post-hardcore New York energy? It's hella aggro. Like, are we going to fight or fuck? Like, what's going to happen here? I just needed to know.

Honey C: Yeah. And that's when I met you [Maya] because she had also been telling me about you. She's like, "No, there's this sister. And she is like the punk Betty Davis. And she's out there, and I just need you to come and meet her, come to this other show." So, I get to the show, and Simi's onstage. I knew half of her band, and I was like, "Wait a minute, these dudes like rock." I was just like, whoa. Everybody in here is Black—"Where am I right now?" Because I've been to Brownies hella times through these electronic dance parties and never seen any of us in there. So that was a life-changing night.

Maya: And that was where we converged. That was my first time seeing Simi, and that was my first time meeting Honeychild.

Simi: I remember the first time seeing Maya play with that electric guitar. We were like these Black girls, and we were all stylish in our own way, and we were good at our instruments and songwriting. Was that what connected us? Yeah.

What were the things that you talked about on how to arrange a show with the four of you?

Tamar-Kali: Well, we were all women who were booking our own shows, writing our own music, doing whatever. So, when we have the meeting, I remember being like, Look, I don't know anybody. So why don't we, like, come together on some show shit? I booked the first one at Brownies or whatever, I had a connection. Maya did one at Webster Hall. I did one at the Cooler. So it was that kind of

Simi Stone, Shoshana Vogel, Honeychild Coleman, and Maya Sokora Glick at CBGB, 2000.
Photograph provided by Honeychild Coleman.

situation where it was like, we'll pull things together. Me and Honey C. come from that DIY punk rock background. So, we're like, "We're not going to call them shows. We'll call them riots," and any riots I threw, I did the flyers. Same with Maya. Same with Honey C. See, that's the way we rolled. I think Simi, at that time . . . you were probably the only one to have ended up with a manager.

Simi: I did end up with the manager and a band of men, all boys. But I feel like he was pretty down with what we were doing.

Tamar-Kali: For the most part, the shows were very much steeped in that punk rock DIY ethos.

How did your shows get advertised?

Tamar-Kali: Well, everybody had their own fans first, so, like, we were doing that thing already? Whoever produced the show, you know, they were, like, the producers. So, they were paying the cost to be the boss. They were handling the door, doing the splits or whatever, and they would give us the flyers to distribute.

Simi: It was phone calls, and it was word of mouth, and we sold out CBGB, you know, like it was packed.

Tamar-Kali: We were in New York. We were doing our own thing and had our own fan bases. Then, because of the spectacle of all four of us being on a show at the same time, [we] attracted other people and namely other Black women who were curious about the Sista Grrrl Riot show, whereas they might not have felt safe or comfortable before.

Simi: We were really pushing that our shows be safe spaces.

How did you feel within these spaces in terms of your physicality on stage because you were sharing the stage with three other women? Did you find that these performances were liberating to you personally, sexually like in terms of expressing yourself on stage?

Simi: Hmm. Well, I mean, I grew up in a place where there were a lot of beautiful women around. I never felt like I was like the sexiest person, or the prettiest person, because I just wasn't. I was kind of a dork, and everyone was so cool. So, the beauty of working with these three was so inspiring, and we were all so different in our sexuality, I don't feel like there was a lot of pressure; I used to wear, like, nothing, though I know we were in our twenties.

Tamar-Kali: Yeah, I was on some fucking, like, queer feminist shit, like, you know, I might be under some nipple shields in a black shirt, but I felt so comfortable at that time. What I was, was what I felt like philosophically, and I think you're very idealistic when you're young as well. But meeting with these women, I felt like I could be my full, pure, unadulterated self. And it felt so good. But then the problem was that, because of us coming together in certain ways, the spectacle of us brought energies from the outside that were not aligned. It was a beacon for people who were like us. But then it also was the spectacle that whenever there's a buzz in New York of any sort, the things that people draw people in. People started coming to see what

Honeychild (standing) and Maya (singing) at Mayapalooza, 2001. Photograph provided by Honeychild Coleman.

shenanigans were going to happen, like, who was going to get naked? That, to me, turned it into something else.

I know that when people think of, let's say, Black women and rock and roll or punk or hardcore, there's always this "Ooh, that sounds sexy." And they think that there's this sexually subversive thing going on because they're not used to seeing Black women playing rock or anything heavy. Did you get any type of vibe from

people kind of, like, fetishizing you because of your image versus the music you were playing?

Tamar-Kali: Then there were some weirdos at a couple of shows. There were some total weirdos. Some thought we were into necrophilia, and we got some fetish-types there. We probably could have done a whole record beating people's behinds because there was some truth in that.

Simi: I don't ever remember feeling scared. I was trying to be a white boy, like a thin, sexy white guy. I was like, those are the people that played punk. I wanted to be like that. I didn't want to be like Belly or like any of those like chicks. Sorry, but those softer women, those '90s girl bands, which had no Black people in them.

Maya: You know what it is? Here's the thing about sexuality in music and what was different with us, and maybe why we attracted freaks or whatever: I didn't notice that with our thing because it was already there. But here's the thing that's different: Music and performing on stage was, and still is, for me, a literal act of intercourse. It's intimate and there is this energy and sweat and it's powerful. And I think that's true with a lot of artists. You're sharing this intimate part of yourself, you're opening yourself, you're naked in a lot of ways. But I think that with women in music, that sexual energy that complements women is submissive and they're opening themselves very softly to be dominated or to be the soft flower in some way. And that's fine and it's lovely and beautiful. But I think the energy with the three of us was different and we are all dominant people. I remember that some of the bands, some musicians who I still love very much, had a hard time with me not letting them take over the production of the songs. They had a hard time taking direction from me. And it was my music because my music was very three-chords simple, and I played with badass musicians who would be like, "Okay, so she gave us the chord structure? I'm just going to run with it." No, don't run with my shit.

Tamar-Kali: And that's the beauty of us coming together, right? Because it's like we could have a soft place to land. Everybody understood what we were going through. It wasn't a mystery. It's like you try to have these conversations with people and they don't, they really don't understand. They don't understand how you're a musician. You have your credits, and you have your experience, and folks are mansplaining to you all day, even if you know they are undermining you. Your name is on the marquee, but the sound person wants to talk to everybody except you.

Afro-Punk events flyer with Sistagrrrl Riot at CBGB, 2006. Provided by Honeychild Coleman.

Do you think that these performances changed the perspective about Black people performing punk music?

Simi: Yes, yes.

Tamar-Kali: I don't know about punk, but I tell you, what I would venture to say is that the landscape of the downtown music scene where Black folks were concerned looked a lot different after us.

Maya: Yeah, absolutely. There was no and would have been no Afro-

Punk, for one. Like, that's the obvious. But the other thing that I notice, like, when you're in New York City, you see things happen organically. New York is the artistic center of the world, right? So, if you're going to see things stylistically or whatever, you see them in New York and there were things that didn't exist.

Well, do you think that this could happen again today? Like, there's so much that has changed not only in New York City proper in terms of a lot of the venues are gone. There doesn't seem to be that organic "feel" in New York when people meet and create art anymore.

Tamar-Kali: I feel like, who's to say it's not happening? You know what I mean? Like, we're living very specific niche, isolated lives. It's like we were just four people who met and saw something similar in each other and got together. It doesn't take much to do that. You know, they are these very specific intersections that are coming together. But you know, what people are getting up to, we just don't know, you know what I'm saying? Like, I'm sure the kids are getting together.

Honey C.: My band Bachslider was on a five-year hiatus and when we got back together was around the time when I met Flora [Lucini, vocalist for MAAFA and bassist for the 1865], and she has opened my eyes to a different generation of younger bands who are really uplifting each other. She's really taken the Riot Grrrl mantra to heart because she's a lot younger. When we think about what we used to listen to, punk-wise, that's what they are listening to now. So, I'm witnessing her uplifting younger bands, even from out of state. I am witnessing more representational bands, and they've been doing shows with us, like at the pop-ups. I'm seeing more women playing in general, but I'm still not seeing a lot of sisters fronting those bands.

Tamar-Kali: There's a reason why I can put together a seventeen-piece female band and take it to Paris. But the messed-up thing is that there's this history. I mean, if you can talk about Miles [Davis], Jimmy [James Baldwin], Nina [Simone], you will remember that

Honeychild Coleman at Meow Mix,
1998. Photographs by Lora Marie.

there's a long list of Black American entertainers that went to Europe for their careers. It's so sad and it's so tiring that it's still happening. You know, it's like this has been going on forever.

Maya: It's like Black artists are rejected here. Go to Europe, do their thing, inspire European artists who bring it back here.

Simi: And then they eat it up.

Tamar-Kali: I did what was needed in the moment, and we were there for each other. We showed up. We created a space for ourselves that didn't exist before, and that's what you do. Like, that's what I've done my whole life, I think, and that's how we met each other, because that's what we were doing individually. That's what allowed us to come together. I don't have any regrets, you know? I think it was beautiful. It's so interesting how us just being in our twenties, doing what we were doing, can be something inspirational for other people.

I've noticed in recent articles that Sista Grrrl Riot has been compared to Riot Grrrl. How do you guys feel about that? Because from listening to this conversation, it's so diametrically opposed to Riot Grrrl, not simply because of whiteness and all that comes with that, but in having four different musicians with their own bands writing their own music and being in control of their own narratives. How do you feel about those comparisons?

Simi: There's no comparison. There's no comparison.

Tamar-Kali: I mean, I will take the L. The name obviously was influenced by that, you know what I mean? That was my whole point. I was being cheeky, you know, Sista Grrrl Riot. And the fact that we called our shows "riots" because it was an extension of just the philosophy of women not having space in this world, right? But our riots had a super soul-crowd vibe, and we were in the gritty New York City, and the things we were dealing with were not suburban.

If somebody asked the four of you for advice today, like, "Hey, we want to put on a show like Sista Grrrl Riot," what advice would you give to this younger generation of young independent women artists?

Simi: I would say, surround yourself with artists. Like, you'll find your people. But you've got to be around artists of whatever kind:

painters, writers. Don't go after business people. It's about the work. And you'll find your people.

Maya: What I see now, I appreciate, even from far away. I'm in Texas but I saw everything that was affected in New York because of the pandemic, when a lot of people that make their living as performing artists were hit or hurt—the clubs, restaurants, theatres . . . everything was closing. But it created this environment in which DIY punk rock showed its purity, and I saw this from away. Being able to see the imagery and the video from the pop-up shows that Rebelmatic [an all-Black hardcore band in New York] was hosting felt similar; it felt like this gathering of like-minded musicians, mostly of color, just fucking doing it in impossible circumstances, and not for money.

Over two decades later, the members of Sista Grrrl Riot have continued to thrive within their own artistic practices. Honeychild Coleman (The 1865, Bachslider, DJ SugarfreeBK, composer/guitarist/bassist) runs her own media company, 8RM Productions. Tamar-Kali Brown (vocalist, composer, performing and recording artist) is an accomplished music composer for film soundtracks. Simi Stone is a self-described polymath, musician, visual artist, vocalist, writer, and recording artist in upstate New York, and Maya Sokora is an artist and musician based in Austin, Texas.

Sistagrrrls

Featuring very special guest **DJ Gretchen**

Rockin' Mamasita Monday @ **THE COOLER** 416 W. 14th St. 212.229.0785

March 9th

(Eve of Honeychild's Birthday)

Tamara 9pm
Simmie S. 10pm
Maya 11pm
Honeychild 12midnight

FREE! *21 and over / must show I.D.*

Flyer for the second riot, 1998. Created and provided by Honeychild Coleman.

FIFTEEN

NONFICTION

SCOUT CARTAGENA

"I don't think sobriety with Black folk is talked about enough. I'm just trying to find how I fit in like it's my first show now that I don't drink."

I'VE GOT THE COURAGE TO PRESS MY BODY, SWEATY, THICK, AGAINST a room full of strangers. The air is wet and heavy; all I can concentrate on in this dimly lit room is how much I'm not like this crowd. It all seems so effortless for them, but I feel like I'm glowing neon in the dark. It took me hours to stretch these ripped tights over my cannon-like thighs. The flared jeans and sweater I hid behind the trash can by the bar are soaking up spilled beer and cigarettes, destined to be glued to that spot for eternity. There's no way my Black-ass mother would've agreed to this, let alone this outfit. Did they have to go through this double life like this? Or were their families blasting Black Flag and Reagan Youth on the car ride to school? How long had they known these songs, these bands, this scene? I always feel two hundred steps behind from having my face buried in Bibles for so long. Verse after verse mixing with angelic hymns cramped in tight pews—I'd rather be shoulder to shoulder in this bar that smells like piss and Natty Bohs than there. I'd rather be here than anywhere else.

A sharp, sour feeling hits my throat from drinking the fluorescent blue Hpnotiq in the back of an older screamo dude's van who lived up the street. You'll get carded fer sure; just drink a bottle on the way, and you'll be straight. Luckily, some dude in his thirties wanted to point out how "exotic" I look and buys me drinks in between the chest-vibrating songs of each band. Each sip warms my belly and everything below. With a belly full of citywide specials and thick boots on my feet, I can take this room on. I know it.

With drunk courage I push myself to the front, eager to see how the drums are played outside of a church. Shoved to the right, I grip the edge of the stage and feel the speaker against my side. Ringing in between choruses, vibration in my eyes. Can I understand a single lyric? Barely, but it feels like I've known this song my entire life. Someone throws their arm around my shoulders and rocks side to side with spittle forming at the corners of their wet mouth.

"I'm not lookin for a WAAAAaaayyyy out

"I'm not trynna escape

"I don' always have a plan

"But I know what it TAKES!"

When the music stops, changing from one band to another like a noisy shapeshifter, my courage wanes. My spitting-lyrics friend has disappeared into thin air. Someone laughs loudly over the sound guy's shitty playlist, someone yells *FUCK*, and some poor idiot crushes a can against their forehead. In the back, I see Van Guy is groping up a tiny goth (who I'm pretty sure is in my Social Studies class); the rest of the band is nodding and arguing in a huddle about tunings and something about pedals.

I'm too aware of how I'm standing. My clothes feel ill-fitted. I don't belong here. I need to go. You need to go NOW. Imposter.

Hey, wanna do a shot? Like an angel smirking from six-foot-two clouds, they shove a tiny plastic cup into my eager hands and ritualistically we tap cups, tap the bar, and throw open our throats. A burn

a wince

a warmth

a smile.

I could do this all night if I don't have to return to feeling like I did seconds ago.

And I do, night after night, sometimes stumbling into the freezing Baltimore air to puke my guts out by some house cat–size rat before the last band starts up.

FIFTEEN

I laugh too loud, scream my crass opinions over whomever I can, press myself against whoever is buying drinks.

I'm at my best like this, I've convinced myself—fifteen never felt so sweet.

MY ECHELON SUMMER (EXCERPT)

FICTION

HONEYCHILD COLEMAN

"My first punk show was RuPaul's band at Peppermint Lounge."

Ech·e·lon /ˈeSHəˌlän/
noun: a level or rank in an organization, a profession, or society.

T'S 2003 AND YOUNG, BLACK ART-PUNK FREDA IS LIVING AND LOVING her best DIY life in New York City. On a quest for emotional authenticity, Freda navigates social echelons while also rocking out in the streets of the Lower East Side and Brooklyn. Based on a true story, this is an excerpt from the novel-in-progress *Black Girl: Blue Hair.*

ANGRY AT A COLOR

It's understood that I am not
In that echelon

"I hate that you cut your hair like that. It causes problems for you finding a man! It makes me so angry," she said between sips of coffee and the biscuits I had made for us. By "made," I mean I opened up a can of Southern-style buttermilk biscuits, laid them onto a baking tray, and added different toppings to them. Some dusted with cinnamon, gently pressed with sesame seeds, or stuffed with black currants to add a homemade feel I had seen on one of those cooking shows where the host always ends each episode with a crafty cocktail of pantry ingredients.

Back to Sharon's comment, I felt both attacked and scrutinized. I mean, what can I say to that? Especially since she can't keep a man any longer than me, despite her long, relaxed, breaking tresses and constantly finding a reason to drop "but I've got That Good Hair" into random conversations. No shade—I have dabbled in hair relaxers with the best of them—but to me, hair is art and I wear mine proudly. Styling my hair as man-bait had never occurred to me.

Sharon, a St. Louis transplant, had posted that she was bored and wanted to meet up with someone, so I invited her over to my place. We had been hanging out on the regular outside of our LES scene, meeting for coffee at the Verb on the Northside, or drinks at Clem's. We shared job hunting and recruiter advice as we both shifted into trying to work as freelancers in the fashion industry.

Maybe Sharon was mad about walking up the six flights of stairs to my apartment in her heavy faux-fur coat . . . or the scorching tenement heat of the radiators . . . or didn't really want to hang out with me specifically but had no cooler offers. Sharon is tall and thin, caramel skinned, righteous and popular in the Ludlow Street clique. And, alas, I am not. Sharon can pass for straight-laced yet is often confused when she finds herself misunderstood in corporate settings. Her sense of humor is a little acrid and catches people off guard, but I like that about her. There are so many layers to me. I never expect anyone to understand me.

I told her today that no matter how plainly and ABG (average Black girl) I present myself, I will never be conservative enough "in the straight world." This knowledge is actually quite liberating, and once I realized it, I began wearing all-black clothing nearly every day . . . but that was tenth grade. I still embrace my nonconformist spirit, just as I embrace my friends in their own paths and identities.

For a couple of years, Sharon and I both worked in Nolita, keyholders to high-end boutiques across the street from each other. We added flavor to a very pale block of retail shops and would wave hello sometimes but never hung out. Then, I ran into her at a skate punk house party in Bed-Stuy on July Fourth. I biked over on my clunky Schwinn cruiser and rolled into the barbecue alone knowing I would run into folks. If the crowd was too overwhelming, I could always bike to the Northside and catch the fireworks off the broken-down piers below Kent Avenue. But this party was the closest thing to

California backyard parties I'd felt since I moved back to New York and I absolutely loved it. It spilled over into a vacant, dilapidated house next door with the windows open on the second floor and two kegs. It was beautiful!

In the backyard, there was a skate ramp covered in spray-painted tags and stickers. Inside, bands played on pallets stacked up to create a mini stage. In the driveway, three barbecue grills were going (one vegan, naturally). The host, Henry, a respected punk brother and hardcore photographer, was manning all three grills and not breaking a sweat. In the back room on the first floor of the house, he had a big white photo studio setup with a distressed black painted wall that people were posing against. I spotted Sharon out back with a pack of tattoo-covered white girls who skated and seemed to be a part of the scene. We were the only Black women at the party. Eventually, we warmed up to each other with the familiar "(Whas)sup?" nod and eyebrow raise.

Now, on this winter day, I found myself staring at her in my kitchen, watching her scrunched-up face in the reflection of a large mirror I had scavenged from the street. "This mirror is mad janky!"

She hated hard on my "found and free" aesthetic, rolling her eyes more as she reapplied vampire blood–red matte lipstick. She hated that I'd painted the mirror frame canary yellow. Yellow is okay for my Bad Brains T-shirt, but not for the mirror on my wall? I was baffled at how someone who claimed to be a creative thinker could be so angry at . . . a . . . color?!

The wood beams were breaking through the cheap linoleum tiles on the floor where she had stomped around snatching open my metal kitchen cabinets—"You got roaches in here?!"—looking for additional things to criticize about my place.

"The floor looked like this the day I moved in and my landlord doesn't care," I told her before she pivoted to the next thing to berate me about. Rolling her eyes, sucking her teeth disapprovingly at the band flyers and posters on my wall, my record collection, the size of my VHS television . . .

I was genuinely stunned at how conventional some of her

outlooks were, disappointed that the cool sister I had bonded with in Nolita, who hung out in my same LES skate and fashion scene, turned out to not be so accepting after all. She talked about the Fish Bar as if it were an Ivy League club she was super grateful to belong to.

I didn't know any of the pro skaters or scene girls that Sharon name-dropped, and it occurred to me that we were never there on the same afternoons or nights. How odd.

I'm in my two-dollar sandals drinking stale Evian
You know the dream that I record behind my ears
You'll never hear
you'll never stay here again

BEEPERS AND CREEPERS

It's understood ten thousand times
a hang-up is a metal blade
and my hands are cut on your receiver

Leni and I met by happenstance two years ago. On a rainy late autumn Friday night our mutual friend Todd introduced us—they worked together designing high-end messenger bags. That night was their monthly happy hour DJ party. When I arrived at Open Air Bar, Leni was standing tall in high platform sneakers beneath her ankle-length cargo-pocketed skirt. I peeked into the booth after hugging Todd as they were playing a tag-team set of punk, electro-funk, and new wave, shifting between mash-up CDs and vinyl. Leni and I instantly bonded on taste in music and fashion sense. Her deconstructed cyber designs spoke to the sci-fi nerd in me—just a touch of Tank Girl feelings yet something all her own. Leni gets mistaken for Meg White from the White Stripes all the time even though they look nothing alike except for both being petite and, well, white.

"You two should play a set together!" Todd said, after our introduction. The room behind the DJ booth was getting steamy and

Todd's chunky black-framed glasses fogged up, blending in with his extremely pale face and shaven head under the black light. I don't know how he could even see the mixer through the fog, but he kept playing while Leni and I hung out. She and I sat in a corner booth talking about music and admiring each other's patent-leather dog collars. I wasn't so ambitious about spinning—some friends had hired me to DJ at their goth weddings—but I suddenly realized that the idea of doing a weekly party appealed to me. And it would also justify my crate-digging habit. I'm in!

Leni and I attempted to start our own DJ night at a few dive bars around Alphabet City to no avail. Then our friend Patti, legendary house party DJ, needed someone to cover her at Botanica on a Tuesday. The managers took a liking to us and offered us a Saturday night spot. We spin whatever we want as long as the energy is up and the drinks are flowing until 2 a.m.

Leni plays metal and breakcore with rare 1960s one-hit pop wonders mixed in. I play mostly punk and new indie rock and have a penchant for 1960s sound effects as interludes. Often drunken fools will come up and shove CDs in our faces, saying "Put *this* on!" Sometimes they try to come behind the DJ coffin (our makeshift booth) and look through our records. Every so often, there's an indie A&R person who digs our set and gifts us with some up-and-coming vinyl—that's how I fell in love with the Shocking Pinks. Once, a guy randomly walked up without saying a word and just started scratching my Bloc Party record. His friends dragged him away, but he left such a large scratch on it that it started skipping. I asked the security guard to bring him back to the booth.

"It's an import limited pressing, fool!" I yelled at his friends. They did actually feel bad, coughing up a twenty-dollar bill before carrying their drunken bro up the steps and out of the bar.

In most instances when people asked for mainstream requests, Leni would quietly turn her back and start playing Queensrÿche or Anthrax. I would fall to the booth seat laughing, grabbing my ribs from the pain, then tag-team her with Ministry or She Wants Revenge. Eventually we made a NO REQUESTS sign. It worked about 40 percent of the time.

Other times our friends Gia or Tomás would visit and punk rock go-go dance. Due to the Cabaret Law, no real dancing was allowed (thanks, Giuliani), yet they managed to move their entire bodies spastically while keeping their feet planted in place, which also helped block people from getting behind the decks with us. And if one of us needed a restroom break, I had a gig with one of my bands, or Leni's boyfriend was blowing up her beeper, Tomás would jump behind the decks, no headphones at all, and start cutting between Mudhoney and the *Xanadu* soundtrack flawlessly.

Last night after our DJ shift, I hopped on the L train to pick up my bike and rolled past Savalas where my friend Nathan DJs. Savalas is like the Moulin Rouge, minus the windmill, but draped in blue velvet burn-out wallpaper and supper club–style vinyl booths with round tables. The music caters to a mélange of hip-hop and hipster kids with a few art-punks thrown in, and I'm here for it. Nathan is dancing between tracks in Black Flys shades, a Nigerian print tailored jacket, Apollo Heights T-shirt, cut-off white jeans, and white Vans with no socks, Afro impeccable despite the rising heat in the club. He waves hello as I stash my record bags behind the bar, then jump up on it to dance while someone pours Champagne down my throat. I didn't drink much during my DJ set, so this is a nice wind-down. As the dance floor in the back empties out a bit, the haze from cigarette smoke mixed with machine fog thins out. I kindly tip the bartenders and retrieve my bags to exit. The clock will strike 4 a.m. soon and the gates will be pulled down. I've danced behind those shuttered gates enough instances to know when to get out before the barback falls asleep in the booth and everyone starts ordering breakfast from Kellogg's Diner. I wink at Nathan and step out onto the street.

SKATEBOARD WHIPLASH

And it's understood ten thousand times
A hang-up is a metal blade and my hands are cut on
    your receiver
If you won't be my receptacle, you won't be my lover
    either

"That's so romantic," Cayce said, matter-of-factly, after reading my freshly penned lyrics. Uh oh, I've broken the Cool Chick Facade. Once that guard is down, they can find an easy out by projecting anything onto you to make you feel shame. It's another toxic masculinity power move, nevermind that you're having this raw experience together.

I felt crushed that I had gotten too relaxed around Cayce too soon, even though I had no designs on turning whatever this story was with him into "something more." Then it occurred to me that Cayce wasn't entirely wrong. I did want more than the fleeting thrill of a scandal. I wanted someone waiting for me and me alone in the window . . . who likes books and wears ragged thrift-shop mohair sweaters (like Laurie Anderson's song before things went sour) . . . who sleeps in after I've left for the studio or a DJ shift . . . and makes my bed when they leave.

Cayce's head was freshly shaven, so his brown eyes looked striking, surrounded by sun-splashed blotchy freckles. He was tall and tanned so dark that no one questioned his claims to having some Native American heritage on one family tree branch or another. We'd met at Three of Cups one random Wednesday night when he was DJing during one of Gia's bartending shifts. I recognized him from hearing his power trio play a few times at Don Hill's.

Sometimes Cayce would ring me up at 3 a.m. "I'm down the block—you up?" then pop over with his drummer Dakota in tow . . . and a bag of coke.

"You don't really party, do you?" He seemed surprised every time.

Dakota was mellower, oddly, even after doing a few rails off a tea saucer. Cayce was on another one of his keyed-up righteous rants talking about how he would never eat McDonald's "because it's so unhealthy," despite having stopped in there on the way to my place to pick up a juice.

"But you don't even eat vegetables!" I laughed.

Silence. Another bump. Then I heard my roommate Alan rumbling around the kitchen. I too was sleepy yet trying to be cordial, waiting for daylight so that Dakota would leave.

Cayce once told me, "You're the poorest famous person I've ever met." He was proud as he said it, implying that I will never "sell out."

He has nothing to sell, let alone sell out to. The son of famous news journalists, all he has to do is show up in a suit. Not saying he wasn't talented—his band wrote great and memorable songs, and I loved his ideas and his voice and guitar playing. Cayce seemed to enjoy life's excesses with carefree abandon, and his band was riding the high crest of a popular wave that summer.

On another Sunday, he met me at a West Side art gallery where Animal Collective had a performance art installation. We agreed to try something different and "stay sober" that night just to see how it would feel (his idea). After the art party, we walked across town and over the Williamsburg Bridge, witnessing summer evaporate into the chilly night fog. When we got indoors, our clothing felt damp. In my loft bed Cayce left a faint gray footprint on my ceiling where the dye in his new black socks had stained his skin. It's still there.

> You know it's understood
> the dream I live behind my eyes
> Will go unspoken
> from here on out

Leni and I were visiting Gia at Whiskey Ward one Friday. I was just back from gigging in France and Denmark and she was visiting from Montreal. Exiting the subway, we ran into Cayce on Essex Street. A few years had passed since our Echelon Summer and he had stopped drinking, drugs, everything, lost about twenty pounds from his tall frame, and grown out his buzz cut into a dark brown mohawk. I'd never seen his natural hair color before. He was stoked about his new band. He seemed happy.

As I crossed the street to enter the bar, I heard her voice calling their dog.

"He has a dog? One of those little dogs that fits into a tote bag? This is who he is now?" Leni said, equally stunned.

"Or maybe it's who he always was," I added as we walked through the bar's double doors.

Gia came around the bar to greet me. "Grrrl, I know. He was just in here with Yvette!"

Yvette was the band photographer and hometown honey who Cayce would conveniently tell me "I told you about" a few months after the fact. The one who shaved his head in the bathroom at CBGB. The one who looked the other way when all the other side chicks were standing next to her in the front row at his show. That was the release party for his band's video that I had a cameo in, slamming a door in the face of some boxer dude in one scene, then stepping over his collapsed body in another. Cayce likely justified my appearance to Yvette because "our bands know each other."

Once I looked around the room and caught the vibe that Cayce had invited his entire harem to show up and show out, I walked out of the Continental before his band even hit the stage.

> *And I cut my nails on strings again*
> *Say her name and make it real*
> *I can feel it on my tongue like the salt that shouldn't heal*
> *And it's understood that I am not in that*
> *Echelon*

That was the last time I'd seen him in person. Until tonight.

"They were having an engagement party."

Two margaritas awaited us, with salt.

NO WHITES ON THE MIC

ROUNDTABLE

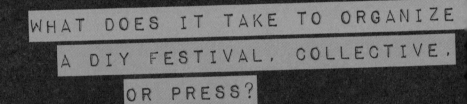

WHAT DOES IT TAKE TO ORGANIZE A DIY FESTIVAL, COLLECTIVE, OR PRESS?

What does it take to organize a DIY festival, collective, or press? What's difficult and/or thrilling about the work that each of you do?

SHANNA
People go to the shows, and they think this is really fun, but they don't realize how much work actually goes behind it to book bands, to get fans to come to find the space, to find a space that everybody agrees with, to make sure that the people who have the space align with your own personal politics, finding money to book a venue . . . It's just a lot. A lot goes into it.

COURTNEY
Christina, back me up. I would say it takes time and effort, especially when you have a full-time job. You can't do this on the side, you really have to make time for it. For me, especially working full-time, it's a way to have a creative outlet. It's work, it's tiring, but it doesn't feel like work.

CHRISTINA
The day job is a big part of our practice. I do run two other businesses outside of #Blkgrlswurld. One of them is a tech company, so I basically funnel money from the tech company into projects like #Blkgrlswurld.

SCOUT

I put all my money into the first year of Break Free Fest. I worked a $7.50 job at Lush and was just throwing any money I could into paying for the fest. I wanted to create a space where the bands got paid and the rest of the money went towards organizations we think deserve it.

SHAWNA

I'm one person. I don't know if y'all felt this way, but I feel like people were coming to me with their emotions and problems and wanting me to resolve their dramas and traumas. You know, Black women, or those perceived as Black women, have that kind of expectation.

SCOUT

100 percent on that. The first year, it was literally just me and my roommate, that's it. I was the one talking to venues, I was the one helping to book bands, I was on "security"—it was just us and our friend. I was the one paying bands, sometimes pre-paying these bands, out of my account, just trying to get them to want to come.

People need money in order to travel, so I got it. But also, asking for plane tickets and hotels and paying on top of it almost drove me off the cliff. I'd stress DIY and they're like "Yeah, DIY . . . but also what's your budget?" I'm like, "Not a plane ticket from the west coast for each of your five members and friends and band merch."

CHRISTINA

We've definitely found in the last few years that some people will presume that our organization is, like, fully staffed. We can't even get our brother to volunteer!

SHANNA

If you're working in a collective, trying to find a common ground and consensus [is hard]. Particularly if you have a bunch of different personalities coming in. Not everybody agrees on a particular subject, or who to book, who to turn to for resources . . . It's a lot that goes into it.

STEPHANIE

Every year when we start planning the festival, we get an influx of people who want to join the collective. Then slowly, over the months, less and less people turn up to meetings. It's an amount of work and focus that not everyone can achieve. Even though a lot of people want the festival to exist, being able to come to every meeting and figure out what's going on can be quite hard. So I think it takes a lot of stamina, and a kind of persistence, and a community-minded outlook on life. I think most of the people that have remained in our collective and are really dedicated to organizing the festival do other community organizing and community work. The festival is about bringing something to our community.

You know, in the UK, we don't have a lot of scenes that are dedicated just to people of color. So, the Decolonise space is very, very rare in that sense.

SHAWNA

When we started the Universe Is Lit it definitely was about what we love, what we wanted to put out there, and envisioning the type of space we wanted to see.

For us, it was important not to be reacting against, so when we made our mission statement, a lot of things would be for Black and brown folks, but there was a whole paragraph about white supremacy and the white gaze and stuff. Then we were like, "We don't want to talk about any of that. We just want to talk about what we're uplifting, what we believe in, and the sense of magic."

We truly believe that if we help to create and usher in this space it is magic. Maybe we were a little egotistical cause we were like "We're gonna destroy white supremacy! The world's never gonna be the same!" (Laughs) but sometimes you need that.

In terms of organizing with other people, one thing I learned is coming in, it's very important to get all hyped on that vision, but also, what are my skills? And what's my capacity? Why am I here? Not everyone's here for the spreadsheet and the budget. Maybe they have, like, beautiful hosting energy.

SCOUT

But also it takes connections. We all know it takes connections. I'm terrible at connections, because I get nervous talking to people. I'll be like, "Hi, I heard you have a band . . . would you come all the way to Philly? I'll help you book shows on the way here. We don't have a lot of money but . . ."

You have to get over ego and just connect with people. When the festival ends I feel like I have family, which is really awesome.

CHRISTINA

We had to have a vision, because people do not "see it" until the whole thing is implemented. I remember one of the curators asked, "Punk like 'real punk' or you just mean 'punk' in a descriptive way, but it's really R&B music?"

We were like, "No! Real punk music!"

I remember saying to Courtney, "We need to fuck this museum up. I want to make sure we book bands that destroy this venue."

COURTNEY

We got the cops called on us. So we did it! (Laughs)

CHRISTINA

Most of the security guards hadn't heard about the festival. After they clocked out, they stayed for the show.

COURTNEY

I knew we had done something good when the security guard said let me go change clothes and I'll come back.

CHRISTINA

She was like "I need to change into my chains and leather boots!"

SCOUT

The first year we had it, there were these really young Black kids from West Philly peeking their heads in. We're just like, "Y'all want to come in? It's a punk festival, but it's all Black and brown people." And they're like, "Really?"

We just gave them some earplugs and they ran in. We taught them how to do a circle pit and mosh. And they watched an all-Black band play. They felt comfortable enough to be there, and we were able to make them feel safe and they made us feel kinda like kids again, just watching them.

CONFESSIONS OF A BLACK ROCK 'N' ROLL CRITIC

FICTION

MARTIN DOUGLAS

Punk music
is the closest
form of music in volume,
attitude, and danger to the
original inception of rock
'n' roll. As Black people
are the creators of
rock 'n' roll, Black
punks are keeping the
flame of one of
music's most
important
innovations."

notes

J. Spacuke '22

I WOKE UP IN THE MORNING WITH THE SUN PEEKING THROUGH THE slits of my blinds and dried spit on my face. Blotches of saliva on my cheeks and forehead from the mouth of the woman putting on her clothes as my vision settled to the sunlight and my return to the land of the conscious.

Latoya's dark skin shined under the skylights as she lifted her black T-shirt and pulled it over her slender body. Dreadlocks bounced in the morning air like the sun outside was playing a tune I couldn't hear. The musky smell of stale weed lingered from last night.

When we were lying in bed last night, she plucked a long, straight hair from my sheet—so blond it could have come from a wheat grove. She didn't acknowledge it; the sensation of finding another woman's hair—a white woman's hair—in my bed barely registered in her body language.

In the time we spent together over the course of the past fourteen or so hours, neither of us acknowledged the fact that I recently interviewed her in my first substantial feature for a major print publication, such magazines being excruciatingly hard to find these days.

I've yet to write the piece, but let's just assume I'll be omitting the passage where we become familiar with each other in the Biblical sense.

As she set to leave, I patted her helmet like I would gently slap a watermelon on a produce stand. She gave me a glance I've seen plenty of times: a perplexing look of infatuation, playful frustration, and sympathy. Engaging in this sexual relationship was probably a bad idea, but I've probably been a bad idea since the night I was conceived, so I've learned to roll with it.

Latoya slipped her soft, ludicrously overworn leather jacket on—I almost pricked my finger on one of the spikes—and kissed me sweetly before cascading down my wooden garage stairs. She invited me to a show at a big rock club downtown, but I wasn't sure if

I wanted to make the forty-five-minute drive from Tacoma. She pretended my attendance didn't matter to her either way but said she'd put me on the guest list anyway.

From what I've learned about her through my longtime admiration of her music (I stumbled across demos in 2014, nearly four years ago, when someone whose taste in music I trust linked me to her Bandcamp), my conversation on and off the record, and the way her tattooed fingers gripped the windowsill the night before, I can't help but think her aloofness is kind of a put-on.

Her dreadlocks bounced in a newly recognizable rhythm as she scaled down the steep driveway to get to her Triumph Bonneville Speedmaster parked along the street. The engine roared with a hunger only narrowly overmatched by the way her lips grazed me as we walked in my door last night.

The liberty spikes on her jacket twinkled in the spring sun as she flipped a U-turn and drove up the street toward the freeway. Beaming in through my windows, the same sun exposed the light blur of fog throughout my apartment, fading clouds of reefer smoke once thick and full in the air with conversation, and later, heavy breathing.

The dim lighting of the Cozy Nut Tavern is making me drowsy, but the booths are pretty hard and the slight physical discomfort is enough to keep me present while Latoya briefly slips away to the restroom. I fiddle with the ice from my recently extinguished Old Fashioned while observing the diverse mix of punks, young professionals, erudite softball dads, and townies wearing dirty Pendleton shirts.

Latoya returns to her seat, glares at me for long enough for me to think there's something wrong, and chuckles to herself a little. "I'm not looking to date anyone, but I don't think that will be a problem for you," she says with a smirk that annoys me a little.

In reply, I questioned her. "A guy like me? What's that supposed to mean?"

"You Pacific Northwest punk rock niggas are all the same. Always in between white girlfriends."

It stung, because I never saw myself as "a type." Concurrently, I felt as though she was maybe projecting some shit onto me from "types" she'd dated in the past. It was a curious comment to put out there, being as though we're slowly draining this bar of its whiskey as a pre-interview of sorts, as a means to find our conversational chemistry before I write a feature on her.

Somehow, I convinced a big publication (one that rhymes with "Drolling Tone") to write a big, wordy piece on Latoya Rose, local sensation turned Best New Music–buzz artist turned bitter and disgruntled midlevel artist turned conquering hero returning home to craft her incredible punk music on her own terms. I agreed to meet her in her current neighborhood of Greenwood, where she rents a three-bedroom house with her two bandmates (the basement has been fully converted to a recording studio and her bedroom doubles as an office for the band's business affairs).

We matched drink for drink, Manhattans and Old Fashioneds like we're extras on *Mad Men*. On the fourth drink, Latoya told me her father was a dope fiend. He went to jail for armed robbery, and when he got out, he never came back to her and her mom. Never even tried to seek them out. ("Just disappeared without a trace," she said gravely. "Probably somewhere in Nebraska now with a new family.") Her mom worked two jobs to pay the rent, leaving Latoya with a lot of time to herself. When Latoya was fifteen, her mom secured a full-time job on the night shift at a USPS Bulk Mail Center, and the teenager went to DIY punk shows all over South Seattle and beyond.

She told me she'd seen my old band play.

"That one house show on Kingdome North?" There was a detectable trace of astonishment in my voice. We didn't travel the hour and a half from Olympia to Seattle for gigs as often as we should have, more often than not because we couldn't get booked.

"Haha, yeah," she replied. "Y'all were a little too sloppy for my tastes. Slapdash." Latoya said Knockout Gas inspired her to find musicians willing to practice relentlessly and make the tightest, most precise punk rock music they could possibly play. Even though we inspired her to do the opposite of what we were going for, I was flattered we inspired her to do anything at all. She said she thought we were poetic in our own way, which was the most profound compliment I've ever gotten for my music.

I felt a pull toward Latoya in spite of her playful jostling. Our conversation cast a formidable light on her creativity. How she uses personal pain and ancestral trauma as a well from which to pull her inspiration. She sings from the pit of her stomach, which reminds me a lot of a very important person from my past. We chatted about sticky dive bar floors and driving 250 miles in a cramped van for a crumpled twenty and drink tickets. We lamented being the only Black face at a gig, whether performing in the backyard of a punk house or in the crowd of a sold-out show in a 750-capacity rock club.

It took me a minute to realize making fun of someone was Latoya's way of flirting. (Maybe she has a significant Scorpio placement, which would account for the endless sea of black in her wardrobe.) In spite of my discomfort from a procession of hard truths and almost-truths, I admired her forthrightness. Especially when I saw the easy smile her eyes made.

The bartender shouted for the final countdown before bar service closed. We made out in a bathroom stall, hands all over the soft brown parts underneath each other's shirts.

As of this very moment, my shelves runneth over with books and records; my walls a museum display of grody, discolored show posters. Notebooks pile on my desk in the formation of ancient monuments. My laptop sits on a dark brown coffee table with deep scratches and dusty glass. My computer is surrounded by more notebooks.

A candy apple–red Fender Jaguar with a white pickguard—scratched, scraped, speckled with drops of blood—hangs from its neck on a harness I nailed into the wall a decade ago, when I first moved into this mother-in-law unit with extraordinarily cheap rent, which I thought I'd only see maybe three months out of the year.

Back in Browns Point, where I had my first beer and my first record player. Back in the sleepy Tacoma suburb where a family friend once told my parents he remembered a time when Black people weren't allowed to live here.

After moving from Olympia back to my hometown, to the little neighborhood across the water where the rich kids laughed at me for being a punk (and most of the dudes from Hilltop that I went to school with did too), I had every intention of starting a new band and climbing the increasingly steep mountain all over again toward modest local success as a rock 'n' roll musician.

I've fiddled around with my guitar three or four times since its wall display was erected.

It's an instrument of heavy emotions for me, but also a monument to the thrilling creativity I've yet to regain since the musical project I put my heart and soul into went up in smoke.

Our band was called Knockout Gas. Mavis Greene, our singer, sounded as if Mahalia Jackson drank herself silly every Saturday night and forgot to get some sleep before church. She was a singer, the caliber of which rock 'n' roll hadn't seen in what felt like decades. I put the words for Knockout Gas on the page, but Mavis brought them to life.

Mavis was the perfect conduit for the types of songs I wanted to write, stories about outlaws and dark-skinned women and the heaviness of knowing the friends you grew up with have either been dead or in jail since before either you or them were old enough to legally drink alcohol. Songs with the raw, loose energy of the Gories and Beat Happening and the noisy, experimental streak of Sonic Youth.

At the Evergreen State College, where I went to shows most nights of the week and woke up in different beds across Olympia the next morning, I was determined to reinvent myself from aspirationally normal strip mall dweller to enthusiastic creative-writing student and part-time rock star. Awash in the electric charge of moving to Washington State's capital city (one with such an influential music scene), I was inspired by Olympia's "go out there and make something, goddammit" culture and wanted to start a band with the other Black person I'd seen around town. Mavis was at the record store, at karaoke warehouse parties, spinning tunes on pirate radio, playing her baritone guitar, and generally being marginalized by her musician peers.

I begged Mavis to be in a band with me for months during my third year at Evergreen, when I thought I would get an individual learning contract to write a full-length memoir about being in a band, but instead I opted to drop out. Mavis wanted to unleash her fury on the whitewashed Olympia scene, and I needed her talent, her power, her charm, her humanity. Knockout Gas wouldn't have worked with anybody else; Mavis was the heart of the band. She knew it too.

We were going to take one honest swing at modest stardom. We whiffed hard.

We heard the bat swipe the air like a desk falling from a window.

We heard the ball slapping the catcher's mitt.

Mavis and I growing apart while it seemed like we were on the edge of a breakthrough was the most significant heartbreak of my adult life. In the corner of the backstage area of the historic Capitol Theater, our first and only headlining show at a proper venue in our hometown, Mavis looked me in the eyes and told me she was moving to Kansas City to live with her folks.

She blamed it on my depression, my need for solitude. But we had been arguing for months about creative direction and the fact Mavis had wanted to write more songs. It was insulting to me, because my words were the centerpiece of the band. I basically felt as though she wanted to be the frontperson, the star (which she was), and the sole source of the band's creativity. I'd be the sideman, the guy who plays guitar marginally well.

"The weed, the women, the booze," she told me, "the constant partying. You overindulge yourself until that point where your need for solitude is the thick cloud hanging over everything. That fight we had in the alleyway by the Smell might have damaged something irreparably in our dynamic. I'm worried about you, but you won't talk to me!"

What she wasn't saying was that she was miserable too. Just like me, she hated every aspect of touring except the performance. The random parties at someone's house after the show used to be fun for her. The pretty white girls with big blue eyes, friends of friends, waiting backstage. Either to catch a glimpse of her or me. Another girl to go home with for a good fuck and a free place to stay. A joint rolled up with coffee after rolling out of bed at 10:30 a.m. And maybe some good breakfast too. Biscuits and gravy with a side of bacon. But that all became unfulfilling to her.

After our final show, we said goodbye on the curb in front of the venue. After all these years, we only said one fucking word to sum up all these years, all these tears, all the blood and bandages. We didn't even hug as we packed our gear into our assorted vehicles driving each of us home. Mavis paid both me and our affable drummer Germaine—another Black Tacoma punk who was nicknamed as such because of his unabiding admiration for Pat Smear—six hundred dollars each for our share of the van, so she could pack it up and drive it back to Kansas City.

Present day, Knockout Gas is based in Mavis's hometown. We have a deep respect for each other's work, but we have yet to reconcile our friendship. Three years after our final show in Olympia, I read on *Pitchfork* the band was releasing a new single on In the Red titled "Mama's Weekender Bag." On the B-side was a cover of Sonic Youth's "Brave Men Run," my favorite song. She hired a fucking publicist to get Knockout Gas a *Pitchfork* news blurb.

Three years. That's how long it took for me to realize our band didn't break up; I was fired. Fucking fired. From the band I pleaded for almost a year for Mavis to join.

I initially felt immensely betrayed when I found out about the new lineup of Knockout Gas. In fact, I had spent some time creating a zine upon hearing about this new single. I titled it "The Grace of God Failed Us," a play on one of Mavis's favorite Gories songs. It was intended to ruffle some feathers, and it did. I called out Mavis's fake concern for me, and the idea that this was more about ego than she was letting on.

The zine gained a lot of traction, to the point where a few indie music outlets covered the zine, the breakup, and the full history of the band. (Which was flattering in and of itself, because nobody outside of Olympia gave a shit about us in the years we were active.) The zine grew to the point where it necessitated a response from Mavis, who said, "What would have been the harm of letting me write three, four, five songs per album?" I was painted as an egomaniac, a misogynist, but sales of the zine scaled past ten thousand, and then past twenty-five thousand, gaining me a great many offers to contribute to music publications because the writing was so strong.

Looking back at the entire situation, I do find myself regretting that I wasn't willing to budge on giving Mavis more opportunities to write songs. Now that she's touring widely, going to Europe later this summer, and is rumored to have been offered a contract with the subsidiary of the most legendary record label in the Pacific Northwest, I've been naturally feeling a little remorseful. Mavis is obviously a hallmark talent, and we all would have benefited substantially if I checked my ego out of the door.

But that door's been closed.

A spark of inspiration shocked me while having drinks with Latoya and our subsequent visits together; they were the sort of artistic conversations that reminded me of why Mavis and I were at one time musical soulmates. At the Cozy Nut, Latoya told me she wanted to create music as visceral as the feelings she felt when she watched pro wrestling, an art form I didn't even know she was into. At the Wayside Cafe in downtown Olympia, Mavis would tell me how we should write a song that feels like the scene in *Goodfellas* where Henry Hill is coked out and running doomed errands.

I think a lot about them in terms of each other—not comparing or contrasting, mind you—but their thought processes when it comes to songwriting and creating. The singular ways in which they produced art. The way their eyes would light up when they talked about a song; writing one or listening to one.

Sometimes, I imagine them on tour together, sitting at a table on a bus arguing over whether TV on the Radio's *Return to Cookie*

Mountain or *Desperate Youth, Bloodthirsty Babes* was the more momentous contribution to indie/"alternative" music.

Clear as day, I'd hear Mavis quoting the opening line of "The Wrong Way": "Woke up in a magic nigger movie." Checkmate.

The Showbox is located right across the street from Pike Place Market, a very literal stone's throw away from the infamous sign. I'm standing in the crowd, waiting for Latoya to go on, right next to my friend Marquise, who is about five years younger than me, dresses like A$AP Rocky circa 2011, and has spread more seed than pollen in the wind. We are united by our pro-slut tendencies almost as much as our musical tastes.

We both smell like the foul odor that only comes from hotboxing in my 1981 Chevy El Camino. Freshly burned weed and vinyl seats.

As I watch Latoya slink around the stage—her hypnotizing body communicating more lecherous charm than Mick Jagger's dancing ever could—I wondered to myself the exact existential quandary so many people in professional fields consider when finding themselves in a similar situation to ours: Are we fucking each other because we're fond of each other's company (and/or fucking), or are we just fucking one another for clout? Can we even fuck each other for clout if we both are in very similar stations of influence? Everybody dreams about having the brilliant punk rock partner done good, the kind others fall all over themselves to talk to. But are we partners? What's going on with us?

An Excerpt from "A Rose That Grew from Seattle Concrete"

If there is any landmark that speaks to the full sweep of cultural colonization in Seattle, look no further than the Starbucks on Twenty-Third and Jackson. This is more or less the red line that separates the Seattle of stereotyped dreams (the one that houses white liberal professionals) and the dwindling history of the people who live south of this intersection (mostly Black and

Asian American, birthplace of the city's jazz and hip-hop scenes, and the onetime home of arguably the single greatest guitarist to have ever lived, Jimi Hendrix).

Latoya Rose, growing to become one of Seattle's most notable rock stars, doesn't throw too much shade toward the espresso version of McDonald's (also a Seattle original, for the uninitiated), just that it's a sad indicator of who gets to do whatever they want, wherever they want. We forgo iced caramel macchiatos and head on foot for downtown.

Rose's story is one of perseverance—one she says goes hand-in-hand with the very ethos of punk rock: Growing up with an addict father who went to prison and never came back. Watching as her single mom financially supported herself and her child by working the night shift for the USPS. Sifting through years of grief, trauma, and identity struggles while teaching herself how to play guitar at fifteen and going to punk shows most nights as her mother worked.

Rose funded the recording of her own debut album three years ago, using the life insurance money from when her mom was killed by a drunk driver while on her way home from work. The singer/guitarist booked the studio time herself; wrote, recorded, produced, and engineered her arresting debut album, *Whose People Claim This Homeland?* herself; and pressed up copies of it on red, green, and black vinyl herself—in an edition of five hundred copies.

In a review of the album, this very magazine called the record "a titanic rumination on the deep shadow of white supremacy cast on our country." Its lead single, "Death Called Out My Name," was described as "absolutely harrowing, a testament to the danger of being a Black woman in America."

Whose People Claim This Homeland? earned the

#1 spot in the *Seattle Times* Critics Poll. Every single critic's ballot (including mine) secured a placement for the album. It's not lost on either of us that before the recent, widespread interest in racial justice, hardly any of these people would have cared.

"Success is the rope climb for a Black woman, while Black men take the stairs, white women take the escalator, and white men just use a step ladder," Rose says when I ask her if she's proud of these accomplishments.

When I suggest her hard work is a good reason to savor the moment, to bask in the spoils of her tireless labor, she smiles and throws an Ice Cube quote in my face: "They'll have a new nigga next year."

The desperate urge to avoid talking about music with strangers courses through my blood hot enough to boil over and singe the skin of everyone around me. Too many humans think music people are all like that one dude in *High Fidelity* (and sadly, not Zoë Kravitz); that all we want and are qualified to do is talk about music. There is nothing I loathe more than running into other music critics or industry people, because much of the time I like talking about music, but other times, it's the last thing I want to discuss. For some critics, music is the only thing. So I casually deflect small talk and music people who want to magic-nigger me by asking me to help them understand rap. I'm waiting out the storm until Latoya is finished talking to friends and label representatives.

Capitalism coldly dictates who you are and what you do. I want so badly to be Sam Jackson on *Pulp Fiction* and talk to someone, anyone about burgers and the metric system. But that just might lead to a discussion on Metric the band here, and I'm not with that. I'm trying to drink my beer fast enough to get a little more buzzed so I can stand being backstage.

To my delight, I found a circle of people having a polite-but-frank discussion on monogamy while Marquise held court. Germaine, in town for a long weekend from his career as a high school band teacher in Chehalis, is hanging on to Marquise's every word with stars in his eyes.

"Month after month, year after year. The thought of having sex with the same person for any sustained length of time makes my dick soft!"

Way, way later than I expected, Latoya invited us back to the green room along with a few other people before the venue kicked everybody out for the evening. After ordering one more drink and giving the bartender a big tip, I walked into the green room while Latoya's body stayed cool and unbothered as she floated back and forth in conversation with other people.

There was a very small part of me that held out hope that she'd save our conversation for last, or that she'd invite me back to Greenwood for a private after-party. Every now and again, she'd throw herself out of conversation long enough to pensively glance over at me, but not long enough for me to properly speculate what she was thinking. Her eyes were the only part of her that spoke to me that night. Maybe that's okay; maybe it's better to imagine someone, to interpret them, than to know them. But still I wanted with that glimmer of hope to know Latoya Rose.

We both went home alone.

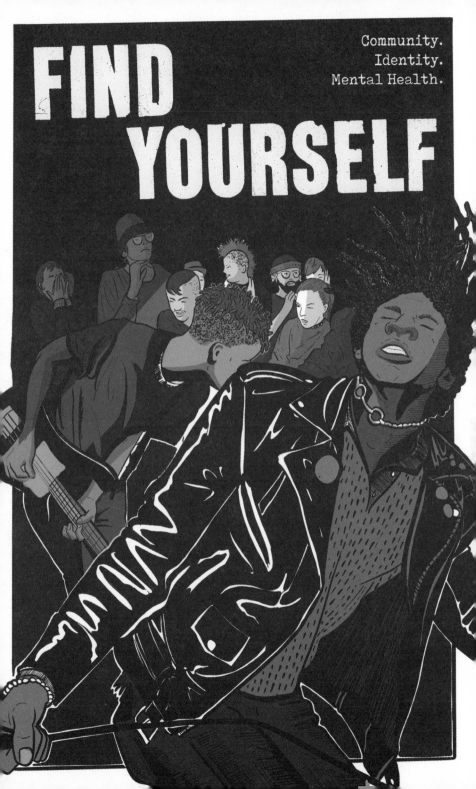

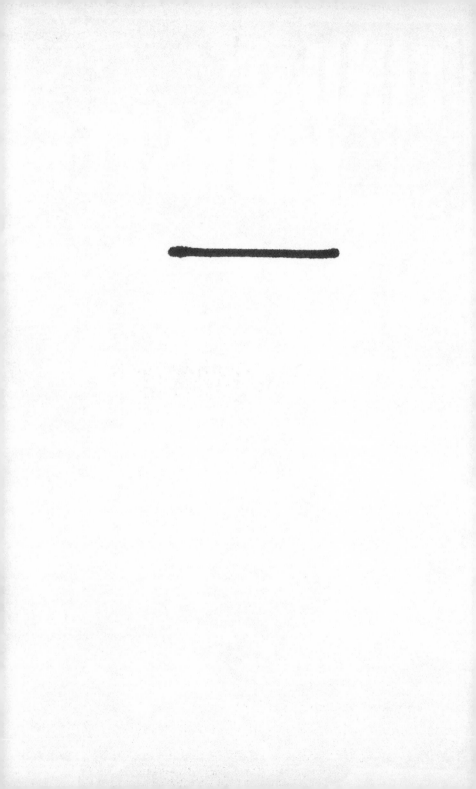

A LYRICAL EXEGESIS OF SOUL GLO'S "JUMP!!
(OR GET JUMPED!!!)((BY THE FUTURE))"

NONFICTION

PIERCE JORDAN

AS TOLD TO CHRIS L. TERRY

"[To me, Black Punk] means either Black people playing aggressive rock music, or performing a subversion of another pre-established musical tradition."

[1]

Big plans! We got big big plans coming up in this mf. Six hands; it was six hands when we came with mathed up off the cuff, nigga and that took two years just to touch ears. I'm living in the next ten years while that shit here. Like, I can get touched before I get to really speak. **Would you be surprised if I died next week?** Many niggas, many minds can get through all 10 years of they 20's with no time. Get a bullshit degree and a family and trauma's still beating them within an inch of they life. Take ten hood niggas, put them in a line. Each be a genius off they own might.

You gon learn ten lessons you could apply. You gon learn what it really mean to survive.

The main mentality of this song is wondering when your time is gonna come. That mentality has been in a lot of our songs. Like the last song on our first album, where it says, "Will I live well enough to be assassinated or just long enough to get shot?" A lot of times it just feels like a question of when.

[2]

Living on Juice Wrld Pop Smoke time, **I'll be in my future, come try to remove it.** I live only for this, it's how I must do it. There's no way they can take what I say and skew it RIP CHYNNA MS TAYLOR AND MR ARBERY What can activate the rage that we be harboring? Aint nobody tryna kill me that hard to me. Like lemme get a gun and you can get it all from me.

I started thinking about death when I was a preteen, around eleven or twelve, after I kicked my thumb-sucking habit. Depression bloomed when I got rid of that coping mechanism.

I was very, very, very sensitive. If somebody spoke to me in a stern voice, it would make me cry. I started to not really feel like I had much place in the world. I had friends, but we would say things to each other that would keep me up at night. And then I had problems with other kids at school. I was also listening to rock music, which is obsessed with death. So, I was just there, you know?

From 2016 to early 2019, I was having a really hard time with my anxiety. When you have anxious thoughts, they turn themselves over in your mind until they get bigger and more out of control until you can't think about anything else. It was very hard for me to function. I'd shut down and turn into a statue.

My therapist and the person I was dating at that time both suggested medication. I was just like, "Fuck it. I don't know what could be worse than how I feel right now." It was a last resort.

I started on Lexapro, and honestly, within ten minutes of the first dose, I felt a significant change. We had a show that night. I remember taking it right before we gathered our gear to take it over to the venue, and I felt like I could understand everything. I could hear what people were saying around me very, very clearly and order my thoughts and focus on any given task.

[3]

How do I remember (they ask) what I spit out the tooth?(hmm) I don't need to make mental notes when this shit is just the truth. But, what matters more, of course, is my resources. It's chores until support, there's no divorcing. **I'm screaming through yr door, "we'll take control by force," and you gon watch me spit the world into the floor.**

[4]

Big plans! We got big big plans coming up in this mf. Six hands; it was six hands when we came with mathed up off the cuff nigga, and **that took two years just to touch ears.** I'm living in the next ten years while that shit here. Like, I can get touched before I get to really speak. What if I die next week?

CT: I thought that last line was beautiful.

Pierce: I was writing this like, "Oh, I'm nice on this shit."

I don't think I'm really doing anything unique in terms of lyricism. I wouldn't say that I'm better than any given rapper, but I think I am better than every punk writer. I will say that. I don't give a fuck. I have never been able to feel like that about anything else I've ever tried to apply myself to.

Punk rockers and rappers want to be each other. I want to exist in a way that shows people it's true. Both genres are Black genres. I know that, more than anything, Soul Glo is just Black music. Anything that we do is going to be Black music, because of the long history that we are a part of and the result of. When I realized that, I feel like everything really opened up.

I've met a lot of other Black punk rockers who feel the same way as me. And that has been the gift that keeps on giving because, as a kid from a rural white town, I only knew one other kid who liked the same kind of music as me and was Black. And we didn't meet until high school!

I always felt like, even if this band didn't get too popular, the fact that we have been able to travel the country and meet people like us has been a huge privilege. That's something that anybody who's Black that gets into this shit has to take a lot of bullets just to be able to experience.

[5]

Living on Juice Wrld Pop Smoke time, I'll be in my future, come try to remove it. I live only for this, it's how I must do it. **There's no way they can take what I say and skew it** RIP CHYNNA MS TAYLOR AND MR ARBERY What can activate the rage that we be harboring? Aint nobody tryna kill me that hard to me. Like lemme get a gun and you can get it all from me.

Everybody who I referenced in this song didn't have to die. All these people who had issues in their lives that ended up contributing to their deaths . . . they didn't have to die. It's senseless.

When every city was going crazy after George Floyd got killed, [Soul Glo bassist] GG and I were in the middle of Philly and there was somebody riding on a bike with a speaker playing Pop Smoke as people were rushing the police. The music's going, "Niggas saying they outside," and it was amazing. I'm never going to forget that. His music was just about existing and doing what you got to do.

These people have so much to give. They really touched some amazing shit and showed what is possible in such a short time, just to get clipped. It's obviously very, very sad. But then you get older and you start to get desensitized to the concept of death. You get numb to it, and it just makes you tired.

[6]

My mind be on 1m, a goldmine worth untold millions. If i get popped before it's clear I'm hot of course there'll be someone to fill in. So **I try to live to fight another day, the way my father say.** Another day to live, another day to give, of myself to everybody that I love and I am fucking with. 5 years ago, we said the same thing

about "today is another day." 10 years ago we said the same thing, but today is "another day." On god I get that and I'm with that, type beat "time stops for no man." I've known my whole life where i stand. People either wringing necks or they fucking hands. I would've hit a fucking lick if I could evaporate, but as long as you live, I live, and you cannot kill me. 30 years ago we said the same thing

abt "today is another day." 50 years ago we said the same thing but today is "another day."

I feel like every Black dad says this to their Black son, because at some point, you have to talk to your child about their anger, because everything around them makes them angry. Everything around them is bullshit, and they can't not see it anymore.

There were a lot of times where I was like, "Why the fuck do we not march on Washington? Why the fuck do we not kill cops?" And my dad had this very simple logic: "You can fight a battle once, but you're not very effective when you're dead. You can fight a battle once, but war takes your whole life." And we really were born into a war.

There were times when my dad would say, "You need to be able to live to fight another day. Your life has value," because I had to tell him about my suicidal ideation, and how it's a really big part of my issues with anxiety.

I don't want to constantly be trying to end my life while trying to live at the same time. It's exhausting.

[7]

Everybody wants their ideology to be the one that enslaves the world. **We just left a century of artists whose screams went purposefully unheard.** We live in the future. We die in the present. I have our next 2 shits in my mind already. We started conceiving in 2016 in a windowless van driving thru the desert. It took so much time, life, advice, and effort to make the first half of this shit come together. And this shit is mid compared to what I'm saying on The L. I was off the Durban Poison dreaming of my mom singing on Russell. 2028 has no guarantee, but I know my dream. I know my Mom's dream. Even though I haven't written I Know Now How Long You Have Searched, I know its power and I can't die before it's unearthed. Everyday we run from ourselves and from time, so much so our planning looks like we've lost our minds. But, our lives are wasted if we don't even try, and it's delicious every time it turns out I was right.

This is me talking about how many artists died young, or had their messages watered down for the sake of making sure that our country's full-steam-ahead direction into fascism is gonna continue happening.

Important people keep being killed by this world before they can really be allowed to contribute something. So, I'm looking at myself as a Black artist who is growing in popularity, and I am proud of what I'm doing, but I feel like I'm just asking to get killed. But am I not asking for it just by living? Just by being here?

I'm not saying anything that Kanye, Gil Scott-Heron, the Last Poets, or even Nas haven't said in a song. But apparently, we're "such an important band." Can't people just say that I'm nice with the pen and our riffs are sick and the drumming is crazy? Can't you just say that you've never seen somebody use Ableton as an instrument? And that Ruben's pedal board is fucking crazy?

It's how people choose to engage with us. A lot of the time, people don't really be listening to us, but are like, "I *finally* saw Soul Glo!" It's like saying you watched *Schindler's List*, like it's your social responsibility to see Soul Glo live at least once or else you're anti-Black. Once we break up, people are gonna be like, "I saw Soul Glo. You can't say I'm racist!"

AN EXTENSION OF ME IN THIS OTHER UNIVERSE:
GAMING, PUNK, AND QUEER IDENTITY
NONFICTION

MARS DIXON

AS TOLD TO CHRIS L. TERRY

"I believe the first house show I went to was Mischief Brew. They were set up in this very tiny room, totally full of people, and these drunk guys were throwing in lit bottle rockets and firecrackers— it changed my life."

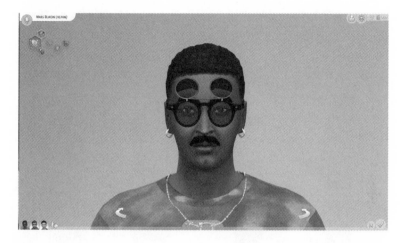

I HAD KNOWN VERY, VERY EARLY ON THAT I WAS QUEER, AND THAT I was not exactly a girl. Video games had a role in helping me explore that.

The Sims was really important to me. I found out about it when I was thirteen or fourteen, at my sister's husband's cousin's house or something. They had kids that were around my age, and they showed it to me. I didn't leave the computer for hours. Everyone else went downstairs for a barbecue, and I was like, "No. That I can just be this person in this other world is completely changing my life."

I'd always wanted a game where I could do mundane things like go to the bathroom or cook my own meals, and then it happened with *The Sims* and just blew me away. I could have a job and play guitars as loud as I want. I was experimenting with "boy names," and used the name Zeke because I was obsessed with the film *The Faculty*. It was so fun because I always knew that there had to be something besides the world that I was in. I was always looking but not knowing how to get to this other place that I was dreaming of.

Then I started learning how to really modify *The Sims*. I figured out how to download pictures and put them into my game so there could be posters of Britney Spears or Limp Bizkit on my wall. And people would make Sims that look like celebrities, and I would have Britney as my neighbor. I'd call her and have her come over.

I started playing guitar around that same time. I saw Jewel on Austin City Limits and thought, "Oh, I can do that. I have a guitar just sitting in the closet. I can play these songs." And I printed out the tabs from Ultimate Guitar.

I had this massive list on scraps of paper. Anytime I found out about a band with a woman as one of the main singers, I wrote it down. If I wasn't playing video games or guitar, I was looking up these bands. I was still listening to Evanescence and Linkin Park, but I started learning about Riot Grrrl and bands like Hole and the Donnas.

It was really hard to find local bands that had women in them. I was living in Jacksonville, Arkansas, and would drive over to Little Rock for shows. There's a place called Vino's Brew Pub, and I was obsessed with checking the calendar to see who was playing, like, "I don't even know the band, I'm just going to go," or "I'll try to find their website." There were a lot of Angelfire band websites around that time.

The Little Rock scene at the time was very metal and hardcore. I did like some of that stuff, but I remember being kind of freaked out because I wasn't a huge guy. Also, I'd known about Skrewdriver because a documentary I was watching talked about white supremacist bands. When I would go to the hardcore shows, I'd notice that most of the people around me were white, and I couldn't tell what the bands were singing or screaming, so I'd wonder, "Is this like Skrewdriver?" I was really scared.

There's this connection between Little Rock and Bloomington, Indiana, and I found out about Plan-It-X Fest. It was just so cool, all these young people converging in Bloomington. And, almost everyone is vegan and has all these patches and butt flaps and ukuleles and rats on their shoulders. And I thought, "Whoa, this is very strange, but maybe this is the world I've been looking for since I was a little kid."

I moved to Bloomington. And I was playing acoustic music in people's living rooms and at the park and just continuing to meet people. I went on my first tour ever. I eventually realized I wanted something with more people of color and queer people and trans people. But it definitely was what I needed at the time.

iiiiiiiiiiiiii

A lot of times, the main character in a video game is an outsider, kind of an underdog or weirdo with a dark past. They're on this journey to make sense of their world and maybe build community.

You're doing that in *Grand Theft Auto*. That game is problematic, for sure. There's definitely some transphobic and misogynist stuff in there. But, in it, you either just got out of jail, or you just got here from another country, and you're trying to find your place. You're meeting a bunch of people and there's this underground, illegal stuff that you're doing.

I created my YouTube channel Wii_Gay to bring people together. I want us to have fun and explore and learn things about ourselves. And not just blow things up.

I mean, blowing things up is fun too.

Before the pandemic, I was having friends who don't identify as gamers guest on Wii_Gay. I wanted to bring them into the world of video games, because I feel like there is a lot of potential for other people to be curious, use their imaginations, learn things about themselves, and explore new things that maybe they wouldn't necessarily feel safe doing out in the real world.

When I'm creating my characters in different games, I usually want them to look somewhat like me, based on the limitations of the game. It used to be that the only customization available in games was choosing names. I was experimenting with "tough guy names" too, and some of my chosen names were Cesspool and Roadkill when I played *Road Rash*. There was a boy I knew from school who was Chinese and Black and I used his name for some basketball character customizations and the Tony Hawk games too.

Now, I always make my characters have darker skin. I'm not ever making a white person. I figure out, do they have curly hair available in this character customization? Or glasses?

Sometimes, when I'm picking the outfits and trying to find something that I would wear, I find something that I want to wear, but I don't know if I'm ready to yet. I will use a game to pick clothes that I want to wear in real life but don't quite feel comfortable just yet.

It makes me feel more like me. If my glasses got knocked off in the game, I'd be really sad. Maybe I'm taking it a little too seriously, but I'm putting so much effort into making the person look just how I want them to, making them look and feel like me, it feels like an extension of me in this other universe.

ııııııııııııııı

There is a good number of trans people and queer people and people of color putting those identities in the center of the games they're making. And there's the Game Devs of Color Expo that happens every year, up in Harlem.

As a kid, I would never have thought that there would be a community of Black and brown game developers who are making indie games outside of—and sort of in spite of—the corporate system. People like Catt Small, Danielle Brathwaite-Shirley, and Robert Yang. I always thought that the people making the games had to have certain qualifications. Nowadays, if you want to make a game, you can do it on your computer. You don't have to wait for permission.

ııııııııııııııı

So, something that people do with *The Sims* is they remake music videos inside the game. I was looking at that on YouTube and saw a related video, which was someone playing WWE 2K and they had the Rock and Stone Cold Steve Austin sashaying down the runway to the ring, very gayly. They were opening up the ring for each other and walking around, so effeminate, and it cracked me up so hard. I was like, "Wow, I want to buy this game just to be able to do that. Just to see the Rock swishing his hips."

I ended up buying the game and saw how expansive the character creation is. I decided I was going to make me and that I'd be the one doing the sashaying.

I don't even do the wrestling part of the game. I love wrestling, I grew up on wrestling, but that's not the part that I'm interested in. The customization is limitless, the hairdos, the skin color, the body types . . . You can go through and have huge forearms, but tiny biceps or the other way around. You can change the head shape and

how close together the eyes are. You can really get into these minute details. That's the part that's interesting.

I recently started playing *The Sims 4*, and now I'm not only making a queer household where I'm in a throuple with a hunky unibrow boyfriend and a cool smart girlfriend but I'm also making a whole queer neighborhood! When you start a *Sims* game, there are a bunch of default characters, and I deleted all of them except one family that's based on the original *Sims* family, the Goths—the dad is named Mortimer Goth. I wanted to see my people in the game instead. I just want my neighbors to be my friends. Now, I have houses of sloppy white queer sibling punks, gay bears, two stylish nerdy Black women, a single nice gray-haired senior man, and I'm working on making a house of queer cosplay dorks.

There is also a master list of disability mods you can add to *The Sims*, made by people outside of the game's development team. As a person with arthritis, who is supposed to always wear an ankle brace, I find it really beautiful that people are making hearing aid mods, leg braces, vitiligo, prosthetics, and more to have Sims that represent them. There's not yet a functional wheelchair mod, but I'm hoping that changes so I can put the Sim I made of my friend in his cool purple wheelchair.

Part of me is longing to see someone like me in the media or in video games or on TV shows. Well, there's part of me that does want that and part of me that doesn't, because I want to protect the freaks and the weirdos. I don't want the masses to know about us. I want to keep us safe and hidden.

FICTION

CAMILLE A. COLLINS

"Punk is love, caring
and community,
starting first and
foremost with love of
one's self."

I.

THEY INVITED ME TO MY OWN BEATING LIKE GENTEEL SOUTHERN ladies planning an afternoon of bridge and sweet tea: with a cordial phone invitation to meet up on Sunday. I tried not to sound too geeked up when the phone rang and Mom said Kerri was on the line, but of course I'd been hoping for their call.

We'd moved from our respectable apartment in Coronado to a scuzzy area of San Diego after the landlord methodically ratcheted up the rent. This meant a new school and an abrupt end to seeing my closest friend every day. The meetup marked my first trip back to Nado in the two months since we'd left.

"We haven't seen you in so long! Come over to my place around two—it'll be so much fun!"

It was a quick call, sure, but Kerri's tone was strangely woman-ish, her words subtly rehearsed. It was odd that the call came from her and not Alexis. I generally tolerated Kerri because, as one of only two Black kids in my grade and five in the entire school, I had very little control over anything.

Two years before, we still had baby fat on our faces when Kerri accused me of kicking her cat during a sleepover. "I saw you with my own eyes! You stuck your foot out on purpose and kicked Mimi when she walked by!"

I was stunned by her capacity to make me out to be a cat-kicking ogre, when I'd done nothing of the kind, and I ran to the bathroom, crying. My stubborn absence finally convinced the girls to go easy.

It clicked after the fact. Alexis and I snuck out one night to see Black Flag without telling Kerri. It had to be faced; she was a simple, top-40 radio girl who never showed much interest in punk, but I figured she accused me of kicking the cat because she was mad about being left out. Maybe she wanted to hint to Alexis that I wasn't such a savory companion after all. That was the demarcation where I started to count Kerri as one of *Alexis's* friends—not mine. Still, I was happy to get the call because, at that moment, they were all I had.

II.

Mother was a beauty queen in Birmingham, deflecting accusations of delusion her whole life, but living in California had been a childhood dream. "I'm done losing," she said, packing us into her old Cadillac, vowing never to be caught dead at a fish fry in the Bip ever again. I bought into her bravado then but in time realized it wasn't fearlessness, but heartbreak over Aunt Vonne, that ignited her.

By sixth grade, I was starting middle school in Coronado. Peering down from the bridge that connected the island to San Diego, the surrounding waters were a glistening jewel. The town itself felt freer and more friendly than our old neighborhood in Birmingham.

I don't recall exactly how Alexis and I became friends, I only know it wasn't long before we'd morphed into a single shadow, one child indistinguishable from the next. Awash in the lucent violet of this new moment, I've no doubt I took its beauty for granted.

"Come on, dork!" Alexis beckoned, mocking my fear of treading too far out to sea. The flash of her smile and sunrise aura seemed to set her in dappled neon as she laughed at me. Whether we were risking an ocean depth that exceeded my prowess, or our bodies were reverberating with the thrill of an explosive live punk band, those days with Alexis were my first sighting of that heartrending lavender aura. I alone could perceive the wondrous beam that washed and salvaged me, while also laying bare my doubt; abandoning me in nothing but flesh and ravaged armor.

III.

I was fourteen and in eighth grade, the very same age as George Stinney, when I learned he was the youngest person ever sentenced to death in America. He was so small the electric chair helmet slid around his head and they had to make adjustments before blasting the poor kid to kingdom come. The idea that a young Black boy would have brutally killed two white girls for no reason must have been just as preposterous to the people who wrongfully charged him as it was to anyone else with a single brain cell—but, as I wrote in my first history paper, "being Black means being expendable in America."

I got a D on the paper. My history teacher, Mrs. Sneed, asked to see me after class. "It's a solid paper, Essie, but I just can't get past the last sentence. It's a very jarring remark and we talked so much about grounding things in fact. Please keep facts, dates, and statistics in mind next time. I think you'll be much happier with your grades if you do."

It's not very punk to be a crying mush, but I was proud to have an original topic for my Black History Month essay. Everyone else was writing about Martin Luther King Jr. or Rosa Parks. "But I worked so hard on it," I sniffed. Mom was chopping tomatoes for our taco supper as I explained about the line that had offended Mrs. Sneed and cost me a better grade. Mom rested half a tomato on the cutting board and turned to face me. "I'm sorry, Essie. It was a beautiful, intelligent essay, babe, no matter what anyone says. They just don't see it, because they don't want to; don't have to . . . I don't know, but better you get used to it so you're not constantly disappointed."

Despite being majorly bummed over my grade, I was proud of my daring choice of a subject. It was easier to confront my mother's forbidden topic of conversation through a stranger like George, and the reaper that chased me for inheriting her fears, than tempt her anger by questioning her about Aunt Vonne.

Yvonne was my mother's little sister, the daughter Grandad had with his second wife. Their age difference was so vast, Vonne, as they called her, was almost like another kid to my mom. She'd been an auroral spark whose presence seemed a new chance at life for the family. Even after so many years, her spirit was a faded sorrow, hanging on us like a blanket from a family chest, weighted in notes of cedar and myrrh.

Mommy, who was usually buoyant with a heart as light as a dove's, turned gravely cold at nearly any mention of her mislaid baby sis. I was eight and dead asleep when the police came. Over time, I gathered enough snippets of old folks' talk and mother's miniature poems of grief to convince myself I'd heard it all.

There was a party of some sort. Vonne "shouldn't have ever been within a million miles of those dogs," because "she wasn't ever self-conscious or half as stuck-up as she ought to have been, kind, pretty thing she was." For "she was a lost princess without a throne, that's all."
  "Sweet as cotton candy and never meaning nobody no harm."
  "No, never. Not a soul!"

At some point this gang of "dogs" deliberately isolated her from her friends "and went at her like hell hounds" but "she fought! Don't forget that! She fought her heart out! Child died with clumps of hair in her hand and pigs' flesh beneath her nails. Lord, have mercy . . ."
  "Yes, that's right. She sure did."

I couldn't unhear the story of my aunt's fate, and I became convinced that her demise snaked my neck in an amulet of fated poison. Selfishly, I relished the morbidity, like a child poking a dead bird with a stick, or freefalling into the cozy, foreign folds of melancholy; just as I burrowed in my dead grandmother's old furs on chilly nights.

IV.

The noise and chaos of the lunchroom at the new school in San Diego was just another reminder that it was everything bleak that Coronado wasn't. Jo Dee spooned the last bit of mashed potato from her lunch tray, immediately searching the table for her next bite.

"So, what's with that 'Black Flag' pin you had on your jean jacket the other day? You a militant? Dad said, 'Ask her if she's a militant.'"

"What?" It took me a minute to realize she was asking if the *Black* in *Black Flag* was some kind of Black social movement. Gawd! Chocolate milk shot into my sinuses and I was trapped by an embarrassing coughing fit. This is what it had come down to—we'd been tossed out of Coronado on our asses and here I was sitting with a kid who hadn't even heard of one of my favorite bands.

Jo Dee's ignorance wasn't a total surprise. I already knew my one and only friend at the new school was a wreck. She was also too nice to be jettisoned. All elbows and hip bones, tall, and netherworldly pale, Jo Dee had professed allegiance to the altar of death metal. Our friendship was still new enough that I was regularly startled by her appearance, swooping the halls like a wan raven—awkward loping gait and outdated feathered hair matched with her trademark black death metal tee and saggy jeans. You'd think her oddball status matched mine, but dealing with Jo Dee actually made me feel even more self-conscious, as if being a freak on my own—Black and female with zero athletic prowess—wasn't trouble enough.

There were bigger challenges than trying to navigate a new friendship while keeping inconspicuous. For the past two years, Alexis and I had created a footprint of concerts, hand-painted bedroom posters, custom greeting cards praising Black Flag, X-Ray Spex, and the Ramones, and the odd jobs we took to keep the entire enterprise afloat. Now my fidelity was challenged like never before. Was I punk for me, or had I just been posing for my clique in Coronado?

V.

Alexis and Kerri had grown up together from nursery school. At the start of seventh grade, Kerri's father's year-long contract in Mexico

City came to an end, marking her return to the island and casting my joy into the confines of her shadow.

Alexis, who I always knew as blithe and adventurous, staring down life with a bored arrogance that seemed to say, "try me," demurred to Kerri's malignant blandness, and I could never understand why. Maybe it was the juxtaposition of Kerri's gleaming four-bedroom house against the small apartment Alexis shared with her mom, a nurse like mine. I hated to see her light diminished in the face of the island's unspoken social hierarchy. Our near-poverty was one of the things we shared. It gave us a voracity that propelled our ardent wolf gang of two.

That Sunday, I laid aside my typical 1950s-style dresses from the Salvation Army in favor of a Prince T-shirt. I was intoxicated by his talent and beauty and insistent on claiming him. He was ours, yet some unspoken tension intimated to me, as I rolled the scant hairs above my forehead around a hot iron, that there'd be times the community would have to fight to make him our own.

Straightened bangs shortened my face, making me look like a demonic Black doll, but I took a curling iron to an overworked patch of hair every morning anyhow for the steady stream of compliments I received from white kids and teachers alike. As I walked the distance to Kerri's after disembarking the bus on Orange Avenue, I was preoccupied with moving as robotically as possible to avoid screwing up my bangs with melty sweat—as if a measured pace would forestall the inevitable. Kerri's white, Spanish-style house with the red tile roof was serene and fairy-tale sweet. I closed my eyes and pretended Mom would open the door any second as I awaited an answer to my knock.

"Hello, dahlin'," came the swaying, Calypso voice. I'd completely forgotten Kerri's West Indian housekeeper, Donette. I blinked and breezed past her, springing into the living room with a territorial air.

"How ya doin'? It's been too long, baby. How you like your new place?"

I considered Donette for the first time since I'd arrived, withholding my dimples in favor of a tight-eyed scowl. Something about being "welcomed back" to Coronado by a Black woman who didn't live there and never had made it feel as though we'd been mutually sorted into a bin of rejects, and I hated the feeling. I folded my arms across my chest without responding. My means of protest against the many things I couldn't control were limited, and Donette was an easy, if undeserving, target.

"Where's Kerri and Alexis?" I demanded.

"They're out back, sweetie." Donette gestured elegantly toward the backyard; a game show host exhibiting prizes. They were standing on the patio—Kerri in a flowered sundress with thin ties at each shoulder, her dark hair in a haphazard ponytail; Alexis in jeans and a Dead Kennedys T-shirt, her trademark bottle-blond hair falling into her face. Some dark corridor of my spirit sensed something was amiss before I even set foot outside, as if we were meeting for the first time and hadn't been an inseparable, though mismatched, trio for the past two years.

They were both holding their eighth grade science books, which seemed absurd. As soon as I was within an arm's length, they hoisted the books above their heads and began to wail all about my head and shoulders. Was it swift karma for my treatment of Donette? Aunt Vonne's cruet of poison suddenly breaking open? The timid "Hi" I'd whispered had gone unheeded. Strange, for in a sense it *was* a first-time meeting, as I encountered something within them I'd either failed to notice or was incapable of fully discerning before.

More than the tears, sweat, and swiftly exploding tendrils that were once my straightened bangs, I remember, above all, their silence. The fact that I'd committed no measurable offense was undoubtedly part of the reason they didn't speak; I hadn't irreparably scratched someone's vinyl, broken a beloved trinket, or stolen a bike, but more than this, it's likely that they couldn't articulate the odious yet unquenchable yearning to inflict harm—their easy commandeering of my trust—no matter that they too would have to sit with the memory of this afternoon for the rest of their lives.

The goal, I suppose, wasn't to bludgeon me to death. I'd been too bewildered to fight back, and after a few blows, they relented. I made a dash for the gate, heartbroken yet still conscious of my shame, so that I fretted about Donette. I could survive what Kerri and Alexis had done much better without a witness.

My trembling fingers couldn't work the latch (now the girls were forever at my back; just this side of a shoulder; encroaching on my heels with the scorching flames of their breath; eternally intent on doing harm), so I had to abandon the fence and swing open the back door, traverse the narrow kitchen, and bolt for the front entrance.

Donette was nowhere to be seen. I felt no small triumph in believing I would manage to scuttle out the house without her noticing my tear-streaked face. I leapt past the sleek Danish chairs in the dining room with only a few more steps to go, certain I was home free, until a vision of her on the living room sofa with a foot resting on the coffee table, more comfortable in these environs than I'd ever imagined, jarred me to an abrupt halt. I faced her, so that she had a perfect view of my crumpled face and demolished hair.

Donette widened her eyes and reared back as though I were some terrible science fiction character come to life. Her expression morphed from ready sweetness to disdain, her mouth soured into a bemused scoff as though she'd known all along that this would be my fate. A loud, ugly holler rose from her belly and flew out her mouth like a banging shutter. "Gracious, girl! Look at your hair! Your shirt! They give you a sound thrashing or what?"

The perception that eluded me during that afternoon of unfolding disaster swiftly kicked in, and I realized her regard for me only matched that of my so-called friends. If they accepted me, so did she. If they suddenly found me abhorrent, she enthusiastically concurred. Whereas I'd flatly dismissed her overtures only minutes before, I suddenly yearned for her to see me, to see our unyielding connection as Black people—to revere and protect it.

"What did you do to tick off those sweet girls?!" she mewed cuttingly. I retreated from the house on G Avenue to the sounds of Donette's cackles.

I moved fast with my head down, my view of the sidewalk marred by tears. The afternoon added a bitter finality to our eviction from Coronado. We'd been driven to the outskirts of town at sunset and told to never ever come back.

VI.

I slept until the moon shot a purple glow through my window. Rapt by the vision that met my opened eyes, I felt a peace I hadn't known in our new place, until the memory of what had happened in Nado earlier that afternoon rocked me all over again. Crying made me feel wounded anew, so I threw back my blanket and headed for the bathroom. I wasn't ready to do away with the social crutch of the bangs, but I did feel nervy enough to finally apply the dye I'd purchased months before. The color was supposed to be bright, like a London bus, but it gave a muted rust tone instead. I was still happy for the change and already felt a slight distance from the experience that would remain buried and unspoken, a tomb within me, for years and years to come.

I'd gone on instinct given the context in which I'd first read the word, but was doubtful that I fully understood what *expendable* actually meant. Maybe I deserved that shitty grade from Mrs. Sneed after all. I was terrified but didn't see how things could get much worse, so I moved quietly into Mom's room without knocking, resting at her bedside as she lay under the covers with a book. "The boys . . . the boys who raped and killed Aunt Vonne . . ." I paused to sigh heavily. Already I was off; my approach too choppy and rude. I'd forgotten to even say "Hey," and had started abruptly, knowing my question would be devoured quickly by fear if I hadn't. "Were they . . . white?"

My shoulders instantly fell, as though holding in my question for so long had been akin to holding in air. After making the dirty inquiry that had lain close to my heart for what seemed an eternity, I immediately leaned away, even though Mom had never once hit me. I waited for her to scream or banish me from the bedroom. Instead, she turned slowly, with a nod of acknowledgment, as though she'd predicted this very moment.

I had to know because that's how I'd always pictured them: a gang of boys who never seem to see anyone but themselves, chasing a pickup truck and quickly jumping in back, their sins masked by exaggerated laughter and the breeziness borne of knowing exactly where things stood. Not only had I always imagined it this way, I kind of hoped for it too, just as I'd begun to romanticize the safety net of a "home" back in Alabama, and "a place of our own," even though I knew there was no such place.

"No," she said, laying down her book to eye me square. "They were just as Black as you or I."

I lowered my eyes, scanning the carpet as if something enthralling were to be found in its pattern. "So, that *is* what it means then?" I said. And because she always knew, even when I hated it, Mother said, "To those monsters? Unfortunately, yes."

It was my turn to be enraged. I glared at Mom, infuriated by her inability to protect me, or alter truths to which I'd already known the fetid answer long before asking. I rose from her bed and stalked away, feeling as though there wasn't so much as one star in the firmament fortified well enough for sheltering grace.

VII.

Jo Dee was waiting by my locker Monday morning, a determined look on her face.

"Looks like I'll be reincarnated as an actual raven before you ever invite me over to play me some of your militant music."

I'd explained to Jo Dee that Black Flag had nothing to do with Black people, and *militant* quickly became our code word for punk.

"So," she continued, "I stopped by your locker to let you know I'm coming over one day after school this week."

"Cool." I smiled.

"Great. It's all set then. Your hair looks really rad by the way!" Jo Dee called over her shoulder as she headed down the hall. I was happy to have a new friend but was hesitant to rely on her or anyone. *Better you get used to it so you're not constantly disappointed . . .*

I went home that afternoon feeling a lot better about life than I had when the day started. Still, the bathroom mirror became a ready altar where I could see myself in a manner I feared no one else ever would. "Ready, steady, go," I said out loud. With both terror and relief I hacked off my bangs so that a mini patch of cinnamon-colored hair ran the width of my forehead like the worn bristles of an old brush. The effect was hideous, but I was happier being ugly on my own terms. I didn't trust myself to simply comb the bangs away from my face—I knew I'd just comb them back down again when I was feeling insecure. I had to toss the entire crutch out the window while I had the steel.

Next, I sat down at my desk and wrote *Being Black means being expendable in America* on two pieces of paper and stuffed them into two separate, stamped envelopes addressed to Kerri and Alexis, with no return address. I'd drop them in the post the next morning. I didn't care that they would have no idea what it meant.

What'd happened to me was a stellar distance from the unthinkable malice that had befallen poor George Stinney and our bereft she-ghost, Aunt Vonne, who I'd come to slyly resent, as if some twisted resolution could be found in placing blame at her grave—but I could see a connecting thread I'd never even known about before, and I longed to return to that innocent state of unknowing.

I turned on Prince's *1999* and began to dance. *Say say two thousand zero zero party over, oops, out of time . . .* I closed my eyes, desperate to conjure the glorious moon glow of other nights. I was surprised by the warm expanse that rose from my toes, swirled my head, and warmed my soul—flickering sparks of magenta and gold—rising and bedecking me so freely, so easy, like air. In that moment, it seemed as if that fated amulet might fly open and be relieved of its venom, but I made believe I held it between my thighs, squeezing as tightly as I could; while it was baneful and pestilent, it also seemed a ready compass, forecasting my direction, and I feared that without it, I might be lost.

NO WHITES ON THE MIC

ROUNDTABLE

TALK ABOUT ANGER AND RAGE IN PUNK MUSIC, RACE, AND GENDER

Can we talk about anger and rage and its associations with punk music, race, and gender?

SHANNA

In terms of rage, I think punk is probably the only musical avenue, besides hip-hop, that really adequately expresses Black rage. It really adequately expresses all that our ancestors been through, because I feel like rock music really just honestly channels all of that. It channels oppression and hostility towards the status quo.

If you're Black and you get into a mosh pit, it allows you to release everything that you've been upset over. And after you come out of it, you feel like you could conquer the world. It's just so liberating to me. Black music has its different avenues and what emotions you can express. I think punk is the best way to channel our collective rage.

MONIKA

I think that Black women in the scene already have this association of being angry and mad. When that does come out, I find that even within subcultural spaces, the same grace extended to angry, raging, white boys is not extended towards Black women. I think that's probably why it's so essential for us to have our own spaces. Our rage can also be expressed without any worries of being policed by other people telling you to calm down.

I'm thinking about that Poly Styrene documentary that just came out. How she was completely misunderstood in her circles. There was one scene in the movie where they were talking about her going to one of the members of the Sex Pistols' house and they completely ignored her, to the point where she went to the bathroom and shaved her head. And people just thought that she was even more crazy. Even though she had done so much for that scene, they just kind of disregarded her.

SCOUT

I might need to just beat the shit out of young Scout who thought Riot Grrrls were everything. I loved what they did, but a lot of times I got pushed into a false sense of security with white punk feminists. I trusted them up to a few years ago because I thought we were fighting the same battle, but woke up when they dropped my ass like a rock for their own good.

I have a bone to pick with the idea that I'm supposed to immediately join hands with white femme punks, female punk or cis women punks because we're both fighting for equality as far as gender goes. And that goes into even white queers. A lot of the time, their support [of us] wavers. I've always felt that way.

Yeah, we're all misfits. That's why we're into this kind of music. We're all the kids who were different. But I'm telling you real quick, that suburban white boy who loves Turnstile ain't my friend.

STEPHANIE

Growing up in the UK, there's a lot of stereotypes associated with Black women. Who you're supposed to be and what you're supposed to be. It can feel very restrictive but that's why I always loved punk. I always find it confusing that people thought it was white or I shouldn't be listening to it. Whenever I put on any punk music or heavy guitars and drums or listened to Poly Sterene as a teenager, I felt like I could get out all of the anxiety and emotion that was inside of me.

I'm Black. Of course, I'd be into punk. Because who else needs to get things out like this? You know, we really need to get out our feelings in this way. Like no one else really.

FLORA FROM MAAFA
(IT TAKES A TRIIIBE)
COMIC

RAEGHAN BUCHANAN AND
FLORA-MORENA FERREIRA LUCINI

"Black punk is recapturing our place in rock 'n' roll music and denying some of the more rigid social and musical boundaries that can surround punk."
    —Raeghan

J Spooner 22

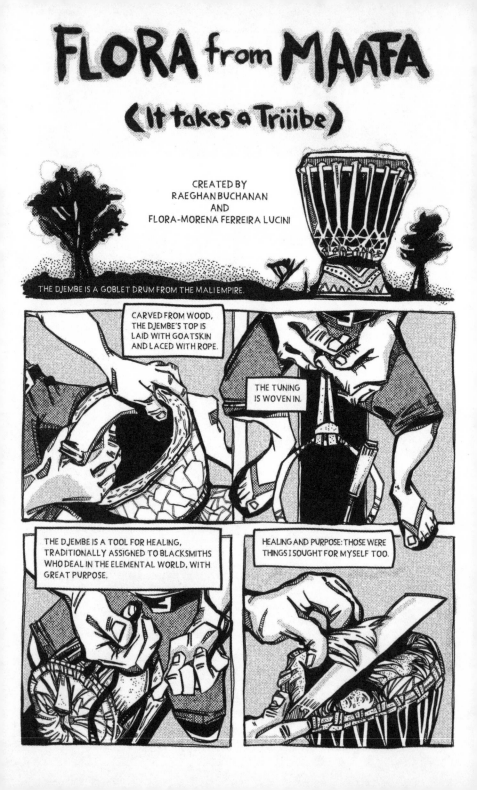

FLORA from MAAFA

(It takes a Triiibe)

CREATED BY
RAEGHAN BUCHANAN
AND
FLORA-MORENA FERREIRA LUCINI

THE DJEMBE IS A GOBLET DRUM FROM THE MALI EMPIRE.

CARVED FROM WOOD, THE DJEMBE'S TOP IS LAID WITH GOATSKIN AND LACED WITH ROPE.

THE TUNING IS WOVEN IN.

THE DJEMBE IS A TOOL FOR HEALING, TRADITIONALLY ASSIGNED TO BLACKSMITHS WHO DEAL IN THE ELEMENTAL WORLD, WITH GREAT PURPOSE.

HEALING AND PURPOSE: THOSE WERE THINGS I SOUGHT FOR MYSELF TOO.

*IN IDEOLOGY-ANTIRACIST SKINHEAD CULTURE WAS, WELL, ANTIRACIST. BUT IN MY AREA, CLEARLY NOT DEVOID OF REGULAR DEGULAR MICROAGGRESSION.

IN 2018, I BOOKED A SHOW AT SILENT BARN THAT UNINTENTIONALLY BECAME A FIVE-BAND SHOW, WITH ALL BLACK BANDS. FOUR OUT OF FIVE WERE FRONTED BY WOMEN. IT WAS THEN WE REALIZED WE COULD SUSTAINABLY RELY ON EACH OTHER.

LIKE, FOR SHOWS... AND SUPPORT. BLACK CENTERED. THAT'S HOW THE BANDS THE 1865, REBELMATIC, AND MY BAND MAAFA STARTED A SUB-SCENE OF OUR OWN. IT WAS THE BIRTH OF WHAT WE BEGAN TO CALL "THE TRIIIBE."

LIGHT'S GROOVE

FICTION

CHRIS L. TERRY

"My first show was Four Walls Falling, Damn Near Red, and Frodus at Twisters in Richmond, VA, March 1995."

J. Spooner 22

THE SKATEBOARD TAIL SMACKS THE DAMP PAVEMENT, SOUND EATEN by leftover rain. The board and its teenage pilot fly over a manhole cover. The wheels hit the ground and the skater smiles, straightening his back leg into the street, streaking off through the leaden afternoon. In his hand, *Rock for Light* is a flat black circle, dressed in white paper, nested inside a butter-yellow cardboard square, resting in a crinkled brown bag, catching the headwind and wafting back like a race-car parachute. As the rumble of the road vibrates up into the record, music shakes from Light: staccato drums with guitar chugs to match, a fuzzed-out comet flicking the corners of the bag.

It's not time yet. The music is supposed to break free on the record player, in the last uninterrupted moments of this Sunday afternoon, so Light becomes a black hole that sucks the song back in. Memories slip silver into the grooves: wet spring air, the blue house that the skater approaches, the effortless joy of getting far enough out of your head to finally land a skateboard trick.

Thirty years later, Light slides down *New Amerykah Part Two*'s side to get her attention.
      "I know I'm not supposed to sound like this."
      "Sound like what? Whiny?" New Amerykah asks.
      "Like a song with a story told over it."

Light scans its body, and shards of guitar sprinkle over the drums before being muffled by a living room's ambient hush, apprehensive parents crowding a loveseat, the skater rushing up off the couch, disturbing a blanket and exposing a jagged rip in the upholstery. His feet fly over every other stair then he busts into his bedroom where a layer of teenage flotsam—a Public Enemy

poster, a haphazard stack of skate mags—has settled over childhood leftovers: a bedspread with a faded geometric pattern, a dusty
toy robot with a pointy triangle nose. Weighing it all down is the
soap-up-the-nose feeling that the good things ahead aren't gonna
happen.

"That why you don't get played?" New Amerykah asks.

"You've been wondering, too? Shit." Embarrassed, Light scoots
farther down, wedging into the corner of the bookshelf.

"Remember when his friend wanted to put you on at a dinner
party, and he got mad?"

"That was awkward."

"Yup."

"But not as bad as the time he actually went to see the band
who made these songs. Why's he going shopping when he's got it at
home?" Light yells and the music bursts forth, drowning them out,
whirling a memory into the air in front of the shelf.

Back in the teenage bedroom and the skater's sitting on his bottom bunk, elbows on knees, clothes smelling like outside as a tear
taps the record cover in his hands. The music, doubled up between
the memory and Light's grooves, is playing just outta sync. Each
snare hits a one-two flam. The vocals leave a grinding echo. The
changes swerve through the air, slammed-on brakes.

"This song goes hard. I don't care!"

Light's nose wrinkles into a stank face as they start shoving and
nudging New Amerykah, cardboard edge jutting into the dining
room beyond.

New Amerykah calls, "I see you! Let it out, old head!"

Then Light cuts through the air and claps the floor. The needle
lifts. The tornado stops.

The music is shaved down the middle, memories curling off to
the side. The off-time smear disappears and the song is crystal clear,
beaming up in circles from the record's spot on the floor.

New Amerykah cranes to look down, "Watch yourself, old head."

Alone on the scuffed wood floor, it's tempting to say that *Rock for Light* is worse for wear, but Light hasn't had much actual wear. It's spent years on the shelf, cardboard fibers loosening, memories pressing in sadness that crackles a summer rainstorm over the music.

You could say that the skater is worse for wear, but at least he hasn't atrophied on a shelf. His face is weathered, jeans faded and filled out, brow wrinkled from squeezing thoughts into the back of his brain. Keys jingle as he hooks them to his belt loop, walking through the front door cradling a grocery bag with a stray collard leaf waving from the top. Surprise stretches his face when he spots Light. He sets down the groceries and, for a long moment, squats over the record while the drums and guitar sputter again, the rain-slick manhole cover glistens, and the idea of a future unrolls.

"Ooh, it's about to go down!" New Amerykah yells as the skater stands, Light in hand again. Fingers slide up a fretboard as the skater eyes the record player in the corner, then New Amerykah's front muffles the music as the skater jams Light back onto the shelf, trailed by a memory of a For Sale sign in front of the blue house. The records slump in disappointment. New Amerykah tries to think of something consoling to say, then Light is yanked back out and held in the air for a sigh's time, a thumb rubbed over the rough salt that clouds its cardboard face.

The paper sleeve slips from the cardboard, then the black record rolls free and Light is lying exposed on the turntable, air tickling the memories layered over the music, peeling their corners as the spinning begins. The music starts. The trotting drums. The guitar's sleight of hand. The maniacal, urgent voice. And Light smiles, feeling cool air whooshing in as centrifugal force whisks up memories that hover over the turntable like a pissed-off cobra: a ninety-minute tape rattling in the pocket of some baggy jeans. The ripped couch on the curb in front of the empty blue house. A hoodie with a picture of lightning hitting the capital. Sun reflecting off a girl's glossy long hair as she smiles in the passenger seat of a highway car. The record needle excavates Light's full, glorious sounds. On the shelf, New Amerykah dances too.

The second song starts, the guitar and drums tumbling from the speaker, tackled by the singer a moment later. In the doorway, the collard leaf wilts and the groceries sweat through the bag while the skater presses into a wooden chair at the dining room table, curled forward and pensive, then reclining with a wistful smile, as memories rocket up, splash across the ceiling and, one by one, float from the open window, pieces of cotton candy plucked from their paper cone.

MYA/MICHELLE

FICTION

MONIKA ESTRELL NEGRA

"[I wrote this] piece to reflect my own coming to terms with punk and my own identity."

Mya / West Philadelphia
Sixtieth and Delancey / Present day

HE HOUSE ON SIXTIETH AND DELANCEY HAD A HISTORY. IT WAS AN old two-story row home that had definitely seen better days. Its paint job was slowly chipping away and its stone foundation was beginning to erode from years of weather and memories. The basement was moist and moldy, the ceiling threatening to cave in, but somehow the house had survived it all. It had been empty and on the market for only a few months, now rented to a new batch of souls looking to find their place in the neighborhood. Mya was one of them.

Freshly transplanted from Chicago, Mya had been hesitant about moving in. She felt partly responsible for aiding in the nouveau colonialism of West Philadelphia, but didn't want to sleep on a friend's couch for the next year. Archie and Taylor were nice, but it still made her uncomfortable to be the only Black person living with two white people. Her anxiety caused her to be quite shy with them, and she would leave the house whenever there were parties or shows. She didn't have to go too far, finding refuge at the 318, a bar at the end of the block.

The 318 was a small, old-head bar, full of neighborhood locals. When Mya had walked in on a Saturday night, the room was thick with smoke and the O'Jays were blasting from the vintage jukebox in the corner. She felt as if every head in the room had turned to focus on her. Her black clothes, piercings, and multicolored braids were not the norm around the block. No one else in the room was below the age of thirty-five. She shifted her feet back and forth but held her ground. The bartender was a middle-aged, short, pretty, dark-skinned woman with an impeccable cherry red lace-front. Her gold tooth shone brightly as she smiled at Mya.

"Whatchu having, baby?" she crooned.

Mya sauntered over to the bar and picked her go-to, gin and tonic with a slice of lime. The bartender handed her a plastic cup with a black cocktail straw and kept it moving to the next customer. By the time Mya got her drink, it seemed as if everyone had gone back to minding their business. She saw an empty table in the corner, sat down, and began to observe. Sun-stained photographs lined the walls, and it was clear that the bar had been there for ages. One photo in particular caught her interest, that of a flashy, heavy-set Black woman wearing lots of gold chains. The woman's hair was an immaculate Afro, long red nails accented slim hands adorned with gold rings, and a red polyester suit clutched every curve of her body.

"I heard that she killed herself. Russ didn't do shit!" A deep, gruff voice behind Mya broke her gaze from the photograph. Neighborhood drama?

"Naw, Michelle wasn't the type to do that," a woman's voice retorted. "I think it had something to do with her daughter."

The man with the gruff voice continued. "Well, they got some white kids living in that house now. Shame that they rented it out so early after what happened."

Mya bristled at the mention of "white kids." She could feel her ears getting hot with embarrassment. She was also slightly intrigued, but not enough to continue eavesdropping. She had her own problems to deal with. Chugging the drink, she wondered if the house was finally at peace after the long weekend bender. *Two more and I'll walk back*, she thought. She doubted anyone knew she wasn't there anyway.

Mya slid her key into the door with a bit of struggle. The four gin and tonics at the 318 had hit harder than she anticipated. She took a deep breath, grounding herself before she came face to face with an entirely different crowd. A cloud of smoke hit her face as she walked in. Punks were languishing on the couch playing PS4 and drinking forty-ounce Cobras. A messy game of pool was happening, with lines of coke being dispersed on the coffee table next to it. Material Support's "Bougie Ass White Girl" was blasting through the house, surely awakening the young kids next door. The old heads will be talking about this.

"Look who's here finally!" Andrea screamed at the top of her lungs. She was a stout white girl with a flaming blue mohawk and multiple piercings on her face. She tackled Mya, almost knocking her off her feet. Truth be told, Mya couldn't stand Andrea. Despite all of her rough embellishments, Andrea had rich parents who had bought her a house in the 'burbs. She worked as a social worker and was able to live a life that Mya could only dream of. Admittedly, Mya was jealous. It didn't matter, though: Andrea always had drugs and the credit card to get the goods. Therefore, they were friends. Transactional.

"Hey, girl," Mya said with a tipsy drawl. "How long y'all been here?"

"I just got here, but Taylor told me that you were gonna be back soon," she replied. A cheer from the back of the house drowned out their conversation.

At the 318, there was a sense of camaraderie that spanned decades. The people there knew everyone's business and watched out for each other, for better or worse. Mya had felt some sense of calm at the bar, whereas her anxiety was peaking at this party. She began to shuffle her feet, her breathing becoming a bit shallow. She had planned on going to bed, but since the party was going strong and her anxiety needed to be put in its place, she decided to have a couple more. She nodded toward the coffee table where two punks were slamming tequila shots.

"Wanna do one with me?" she asked.

"Let's do it, bestie!" Andrea nodded and looped her arm into Mya's.

Mya hoped that Andrea couldn't see her rolling her eyes. They kneeled at the table and poured two hefty shots of tequila. Mya slammed the glass down onto the table, feeling the acidic burn spread throughout her body. Sam, a Black punk with glistening eyes and an impeccable Afro-hawk, handed her a rolled dollar bill.

"M'lady," he murmured jokingly. A fresh white line awaited Mya, beckoning to her to give into the evening's decadence. The room had become a bit hazier, the sounds of loud music and chatter a distant buzz. As she lowered her head and lifted the bill to her nose, she couldn't help but wonder if she had really escaped Chicago in order to do the same things here. The crystals of the coke flurried up her nostrils, tiny shots of electricity sparking in her head. Glitter decorated the smoke-clouded air. She had hit that primordial space of being fucked up but still able to function. Eyes watering, Mya saw a shadow flash in the corner of her eye. It looked like a Black woman, though Mya was sure she was the only one in the house.

"The fuck is in this, man?" Mya snorted, rubbing the bridge of her nose gingerly. Andrea giggled and bent down to grab her share.

Sam simply shrugged as he lit a cigarette. "Some new shit that I got from South. Why?"

"It's making me feel like my eyeballs are falling out of my head," she said. Standing up, she felt a slight tilt in her stance, knees wobbly like a newborn calf. It had to be fentanyl or something. "Ay, I'm gonna go lay down for a second," she said to Andrea, though she wasn't paying attention. Sam had already snuggled up close to her "friend" and it was apparent that they had plans for the rest of the evening.

Mya headed up to her room. The drunken chatter and loud music carried its way up the stairs but was stifled by the thick wooden door, which she locked. She kicked off her Docs and stripped off her black skinny jeans, collapsing onto her bed without even bothering to turn on the lights. She lay there, looking up at the ceiling where a Bread and Circuits poster was placed. Her head felt as if it were disconnected from her body, an odd tingling sensation coursing through her veins. The neighbor's bedroom light filtered through the window, an odd tinge of yellow saturating the white walls.

"What am I doing?"

The reality of her life began to play like a film in her mind. The alienation of being a Black queer woman in a subculture that would never understand her. A circle that would treat her presence as a token accessory to cover their insecurity. A privilege that they tried to escape. Expendable. Exotic.

She hadn't talked to her blood family in ages, so she had no choice but to develop her own support system. If you could call it that. In Chicago, there had been plenty of Black and Brown punks and she even tried to find course with the few white punks who didn't say *nigger* when no one was watching. It was hard work sifting through the trash, but she had managed to pull together a good crew. Sure, punk was a fun-enough identity to piss off the status quo, but for Mya . . . being a Black woman was just enough.

"Fuck it," she whispered to herself. She would try to get some rest and figure out something new tomorrow. She closed her eyes and wrapped her punk patch quilt around her body. The yells and music continued downstairs, but she did not hear any of it within a few minutes.

A sunlit room. The stench of death. Pills and alcohol bottles littering the floor. A turntable by the far wall, skipping on a record that has been spinning for hours. The sounds of cardinals and sparrows in the backyard. Subwoofers blasting trap music on the street. Flies buzzing about in the still, humid air. A Black woman's body decomposing in the middle of the floor. Maggots writhing in the cracks of the linoleum. Children laughing outside, unaware of the horror in the row home next to theirs.

Mya found herself standing in the corner of her bedroom, staring down at the Black woman's corpse that lay where her bed used to. There were no posters on the wall, no sign of her personal possessions, just the naked body rotting facedown in the middle of the room. Was this a dream?

Wake up.

Mya looked down at her hands and found that they were covered in soot, as if she had been digging through a fireplace. Suddenly, without notice, the body on the floor started to twitch, maggots falling off as the legs began to move. Mya gasped, backing into the corner.

Wake up.

The corpse began to shake, as if it were going to stand up on its own. A vintage television in the corner clicked on, a music video appearing. Four Black men in black velvet suits and crimson silk shirts appeared on the screen.

"Lost and turned out," they crooned, and the corpse began to shake violently. Mya was paralyzed with fear, daring not to move from the corner.

Wake up.

"Olivia . . ." the band continued.

The sky outside was dark, the birds silent. The temperature had dropped significantly, a sudden change from the summer air. The stench of death evaporated as the corpse began to stand. Mya attempted to scream but no sound was released. The corpse's face was unrecognizable, her features gnawed away, eye sockets filled with debris, mouth empty and encrusted with dried bile. She made no sound as she began to creep toward Mya.

Wake up.

"Lost and turned out . . ."

The corpse came closer, quivering and dragging each heavy foot. Gathering every ounce of her strength, Mya sprinted toward the door. She grabbed the knob and twisted, but it wouldn't open.

"What the fuck!" she screamed. She began to kick and pound on the door, screaming for help. The music from the television grew louder.

"OLIVIA, BREAK THE CHAINS . . ."

The corpse advanced, arms outstretched and wanting.

"Please get the fuck away from me!" Mya pleaded. She continued to kick and hit the door, screaming for help.

It was only a matter of seconds before the corpse reached Mya, scooping her into a bear hug. Mya was unable to free herself.

"Let me go, please! Please!" she screamed.

Mya had her eyes closed tight, hot tears streaming down her cheeks. The corpse remained silent, not releasing her grip. Her body was soft and malleable, the strength of her embrace terrifying and strong. Strangely, the smell of roses filled the room. The corpse remained silent and motionless. Eventually, Mya grew exhausted and gave in to her unfortunate situation. She slowly opened her eyes, staring into the corpse's decayed face. Blank, emotionless, terrifying. The room began to darken. The corpse retained her grasp.

Wake up.

Wake up.

Wake up.

"Lost and turned out . . ."

Michelle / West Philadelphia
Sixtieth and Delancey / 2017

After being inebriated for two weeks straight, her gut was on fire. The nightmares were calmed only by becoming blackout drunk. But after throwing up for hours the night before, Michelle decided that today would be the day she stopped. Slowly, she emerged onto the porch and lit her Newport 100, the acrid smoke filling her lungs. It was still early morning and quiet, but Michelle could hear faint bass from the rundown corner bar a few houses down. She was one of the lifers that the bar had snatched, and to be perfectly honest, she wouldn't have it any other way.

For all of her life, she had known those streets. Sure, she had traveled to different places, but she always ended up back here. She tried to tell herself that she was okay with the way her life had turned out, but she knew it was oftentimes a bold-faced lie. To her, there was no point in having regrets. You just had to roll the hard six and be content with where you landed. At least, that's what she told herself.

"Michelle! What up, girl?"

She took a long drag of her cigarette and squinted to see who approached. It was Delroy, the neighbor from three doors down. He was a squat Black man with a salt-and-pepper beard and beady black eyes.

"Hey, Del. Too early for any mess."

"Aw naw, you know I ain't tryna to start up nothing. Just saying 'Hey.'" He chuckled as he picked up the newspaper from his plant-filled porch.

"That's a start!" said Michelle as she flicked her cigarette butt into the street.

"Did you hear about Russ last night, Chelle?" he asked as he opened the screen door to his home. Michelle pretended not to hear him and went back inside. The absolute nerve of him! Michelle shook her head sadly and looked down into her hands. They were dry and a bit rough from years of sanitizer and mop buckets. When she was making more money she would have her nails glimmering with rhinestones and red varnish, sharp and pointy. Those were better days. Russ was also a part of those days.

She had heard about him last night. If it were true that he was back from California, that meant that he would come looking for her. The last time they had spoken was full of venom and regret.

Michelle opened the back door. The vines had completely taken over the fence in the small concrete patio, where cigarette butts and empty beer cans littered a sad, cheap patio set the colors of the American flag. She would get around to cleaning that up eventually.

Michelle pushed stray leaves off of the chair that didn't wobble and sat down. The sun was starting to pick up heat and she knew it would be a scorcher.

A cardinal began to sing over Michelle's head, hanging on to the lowest branch of the tree that had grown entangled with the fence. Her cigarette had burned down to the quick and threatened to scorch the tip of her index finger. The bird's song screeched into her soul. She looked up at it, tears in her eyes. She did not want to see him.

Maybe it was her turn to run. Yet she didn't know if running would be the end of the two of them.

Michelle had never been afraid of Russ, but she did wonder what would happen if they met again after the incident. The only thing she truly feared was him getting the last victory from their tragic relationship. Maybe he would want to kill her. Or maybe she would beat him to the punch. She had never thought about suicide, but as the thought crossed her mind it seemed comforting. Standing up, Michelle slowly walked back inside of the humid household. Killing herself didn't seem nearly as worrying as she had expected. Maybe she knew that this was coming all along. She climbed the stairs stiffly, heading to the bathroom. Once there, she reached into the medicine cabinet and found the bottle of alprazolam she occasionally sold at the 318. She then turned on the faucet and downed the bottle with no hesitation, taking a handful of water from the tap to chase them down. Closing the medicine cabinet, she found her own reflection. Her brown face was swollen and acne ridden, years of alcohol abuse and poor diet taking its toll. Her beady brown eyes were sunken and puffy, her curly hair collected into a messy, tiny bun atop her head. She almost didn't recognize the person in the mirror. A single tear found its way onto her cheek.

This was it. The decision had been made. There would be no final showdown with Russ or any haunted memories come afloat.

Michelle made way to her room and laid down on the bed. Perhaps she wasn't running away from it all. Maybe it was life that was begging to escape from her. Whatever the case, she still had no regrets—she had rolled the final game of dice and won. She had lived life on her terms and she had taken it also.

The cardinal's song rang out once again.

Mya

Mya found herself awake in bed, sheets drenched in sweat. There was no noise coming from downstairs. How long had she been asleep? She grabbed her watch from her bedside crate: 4:30 a.m.

219

"Jesus fucking Christ," she muttered, sitting upright. That would be the last time she would ever take drugs from Sam. She ran her hands over her bed, searching for her phone. It was nowhere to be found.

"Hmm."

She crawled out of bed and began feeling on the floor for her jeans. She finally found them, crumpled next to a pile of dirty clothes near the door. She grabbed her phone and climbed back into bed. As she pulled the blankets back up, she realized that there was someone standing in the corner of her room, but it was too dark to make out the figure. She squinted her eyes as she balled her fists. What she saw next made her lose her breath: It was the corpse.

It was as if something was holding Mya to the mattress. Unlike in the dream, the corpse was wheezing a word that vaguely sounded like "Run" over and over again.

"Help!" Mya attempted to scream, but again, no sound escaped from her lips.

Run.

Run.

Run.

"Help!" she screamed again, jerking awake. The sun was outside her window, and birds were chirping. Snores came from the other bedrooms and downstairs. Mya's heart was beating rapidly, her breathing shallow and heavy. A dream within a dream? She couldn't believe it. Her cell phone began to vibrate and she read a series of texts from a coworker, wondering where she was. The time read 10:00 a.m. She was three hours late for her shift. Cursing, she kicked off the blankets and scrambled to put on clothes. She ran downstairs, ordering a rideshare in panic. Punks were sleeping everywhere in the living room, Mya having to climb over a sea of bodies to get to the front door. Stepping out onto the porch, the sun burned her sleep-encrusted eyes, her hangover coming to life as the pollution of the city washed over her. The rideshare was five minutes away. She sat miserably on the front steps and sighed heavily, accepting her fate of a Grade-A shitty day. By chance, she noticed that the mail had been taken out of the mailbox and tossed around the porch.

"Fucking punks," she muttered under her breath.

She collected a stack of mail and looked over it. There were several beauty magazines for a woman named Michelle Kane. *Michelle*, she thought. Crossing over to the mailbox, her eyes fell upon the very bottom of the box. MICHELLE K was written on it, the painted gold text faintly worn away. Mya had never noticed it. Hell, she didn't even have her own name on the mailbox. Seeing the name confirmed her suspicions of what the old heads at the bar were talking about—a woman named Michelle lived here and something awful had happened.

The dream. The terrifying feeling of being held by the corpse, her wheezing. Goosebumps covered Mya's body, disassociation beginning its slow descent onto her psyche. She heard the sounds of the Whispers in the back of her brain.

"Olivia was late, got distracted on the way . . ."

Run.

"Ayo!" A young Black man with a fade and a gleaming gold tooth yelled out to her from a white car. The rideshare had arrived. The stack of magazines fell from her hands as a loud honk snapped her back to reality.

She ran to the car and hurriedly climbed in. The driver hit the gas and sent Mya back into her seat with a jolt. Headphones in ear, he continued his conversation in Oromo without skipping a beat. Mya fastened her seat belt and let out a sigh, silently observing the houses flying by as the driver cruised down Baltimore Avenue. She couldn't help but think of Michelle. It had made her feel as if there were a message begging to break through in her brain. Punk would always be part of her identity, but maybe it was necessary to exile herself. Maybe to save herself.

NO HOME: CHARLIE VALENTINE

NONFICTION

INTERVIEW BY OSA ATOE

OF SHOTGUN SEAMSTRESS

NO HOME

Interview

by Osa Atoe

CHARLIE VALENTINE

is an artist born and raised in London, England. She released her first full length LP "Fucking Hell" in June 2020, during the early days of the global pandemic while many of us were under lockdown. So much of Valentine's creative output addresses material scarcity. She releases music under the name No Home and writes a zine called "Hungry and Undervalued." Years ago, after the first Decolonise Fest in London, an epic music and art event for punks of color, I reached out to Charlie to see if she'd like to write an article about the experience for "Shotgun Seamstress," my self-published, photocopy fanzine by, for and about Black Punks, and she respectfully declined saying she couldn't do the work of writing for a publication without getting paid for it. Since my zine was never profit generating, this response surprised me but more so alerted me to a cultural shift. The subculture I'd entered where everything was cheap or free and all art was created without a profit motive was fading into the past. Now, our creative output may be seen as labor deserving of compensation. The economic extremes of late capitalism are changing DIY culture. This interview is about how punks operate under pressure.

SS: We've been in touch for years now and I always remember reaching out to you to contribute a piece of writing to my zine and you saying that you couldn't do it unless you got paid and how that was such a big turning point–

CV: Oh my God, I can't even remember that. It must've been so long ago.

SS: It was years ago, but it was a big turning point for me because it was the first time I'd ever been asked but it made sense to me because–

CV: I must've been so broke if I was saying that. Now, I wouldn't mind doing something like that at all because I'm a bit older and I have a job, but at the time, I was so broke and when you're in that situation, everyday you wake up and you're like "How am I even gonna pay my phone bill?"

It's not about trying to extract money out of every single thing, but it's this over-preoccupation with survival.

SS: Of course, and that's how I took it. Also, it wasn't just you coming to these conclusions, obviously. So, when I first got into punk, it felt like an escape from normal society even though you can never escape it fully. I moved into a group house right away and we shared everything and split bills. Most punks biked everywhere to save money on transportation and because it's better for the environment. I know you're a lot younger than me and you're living in London, which is one of the most expensive cities in the world, so I'm wondering if you ever even got the chance to experience communal living and food sharing and things that made life easier. Did you ever have the experience of punk liberating you from at least *some* of the pressures of capitalism?

CV: I don't think London has that food coop community thing going on like you can find in New York. I've always lived with my parents and that makes everything cheaper. In the beginning, five years ago, when I first started playing music, DIY Space for London had just opened. It doesn't exist anymore and it was really far from my house, but it was the sort of place you could go and never get turned away if you didn't have any money. The space was pretty minimal, so the possibilities of it were up to your imagination.

SS: I've only been to Europe once, back around 2007 and saw so many squats which is a thing that exists in the US just not to the same degree. But I read that London made squatting residential buildings illegal in 2012 so that's yet another way that the ability to live free has been stifled in just the last decade.

CV: I was talking to someone recently about all of this—about how hard it is to even make music now 'cos back in the day you could go on the dole, you could squat, you could come together and create a collective of people to share knowledge. But now, when you're on dole, they require you to prove that you're spending 40 hours a week searching for a job so there's no free time to do anything else. If you go on YouTube, you can find this video of Alexander McQueen's first fashion show and he's like hiding his face from BBC News because he's still on the dole because it was still bad to take the piss and show *that's* what you spend your dole money on, but it wasn't as strict as it is now. The newer bands in Britain, especially the ones that have record labels, tend to be generally well-off and connected. It's clear they're not the sort of people who are close to the bread line where you're gonna be at the job center asking for income support or help to pay your rent.

SS: And, for sure, there have always been people in punk who have financial privilege and connections, even as they promote this "everything should be cheap or free" life ethic, which works both ways, right? It makes everything more accessible for people who don't have money but also it means no one gets paid. I also know people who came from working class or poor, single parent homes who had absolutely no safety net but still had this level of freedom because they could figure out how to forge a Greyhound bus pass and travel the entire country for free or whatever other little hacks that made life easier and gave them a bunch of free time and freedom. I'm not going to say that's impossible nowadays, but I do think it's harder.

CV: I mean, time is money. Even being, like, a bartender so you could cover your rent and bills and still have time to make your art on the side—now, it's like, "I'm gonna be a bartender but still have to find another side gig to make ends meet."

this city's
too expensive for me

you'll kill me
you'll kill me
you'll kill me darling
and i'll let you

SS: So somehow, living in one of the most expensive cities in the world, with all of the pressures that we've discussed, you've still found a will and a way to create the art you want to make. Increasingly these days, people try to monetize every single little project, again, because of the pressures of the economy *or* because they've seen it happen organically for others and they just assume that's the path. Like, I've had young people who are trying to make their first zine ask me how to get it into stores and how to make sure it becomes popular, you know?

CV: You just have to start. Even when I was making "Hungry and Undervalued," I was like, "No one is going to read this." I'm doing this for fun. I just wanted to take photos of bands. I wanted to interview bands. I wanted to find out how people did what they do.

I made those zines, not because I wanted to make money, but because there was a deep, deep questioning inside me.

SS: You do so much: music, writing, photography, video. Where did you start?

CV: I was always a musician, from a small child [laughs]. I hate when people say that in interviews, but it's true! I was like five and wanted to play violin and then I got older and started singing but, you know how people get about things, like, "I want to be the best singer"? I never wanted to be the best singer, I just wanted to sing for myself. After that, I learned basic piano and then I learned to play a bit of guitar when I was about 16.

SS: When did you pick up photography?

CV: The photography came at uni because I was doing graphic design but didn't like it, so I got a camera and started taking photos. The people at photo processing places would hate me because I would buy the cheapest film but ask them to push it six times to get the right exposure and the grain would be the size of a golf ball. And then with writing, I wanted to be a music writer for a while… I think it came from me actually wanting to be a musician but it seemed so unsustainable to me. Now, it seems sustainable because I've worked hard at it and people in the scene know who I am, but at first it seemed very daunting so I thought, "I'll just stick to writing." So basically, it was like music, photography, writing and then music again. After the album came out, people took it so seriously and it made me take it seriously for a moment, but then I backed off from that during the pandemic. There's no way to take anything like that seriously during a pandemic. You just have to go with the flow…

SS: I was going to suggest that *that's why* it was taken so seriously, because I remember reaching out to you and saying that the timing felt perfect for that release.

CV: I was just like, "Whatever, here's the album." [laughs]

SS: I don't think you have to plan those sorts of things, though.

CV: I had intended to put it out that year anyway, and I was just hoping people wouldn't take it the wrong way.

SS: What would have been the wrong way to take it?

CV: I just felt like it was a bit unsavory to be making music about the particular circumstances of that period of time [pandemic, lockdown, etc.] But then, I was like, "Why am I arguing with myself about this? No one knows who I am, anyway." [laughs] I just figured I should just stop overthinking and put it out because no one's gonna see it.

SS: I kind of love that. It's kind of like a Hail Mary. What you were saying before about just wanting to sing for yourself without any sense of competition about it, that's what I kind of love about the album and your music overall. It has the feeling that you're doing it for yourself.

CV: At this point, I'm like whatever. The way I think of it, I have unlimited tries unless, God forbid, I die tomorrow. I get unlimited chances to get an album right. Because I'm not a massive indie rock star signed to a massive label, the pressure is off. I just want to be low key about it. I never want to feel like I'm under pressure because I need it to work on TikTok.

SS: [snort laughs] Yeah, well hearing about your life path, it still seems like even at the points when you were experiencing high levels of scarcity, there was still a passion to create without a profit motive--even as the subject matter of your album was inspired by those very circumstances of economic frustration.

CV: I made the album when I was finished with uni and had absolutely nothing to do. And honestly, finishing the album felt like a job. No one can tell me making music isn't work, because that was a job. That part of my life is just seared into my brain because I'd just experienced pure rejection--so many job rejections. **Once you bypass the fear of rejection, the fear of people saying "no" to you, you feel like you can do anything.** There's so much relaxation in accepting fear, failure and rejection.

SS: I read that you figured out your recording set up from Grime's blog (the post has been deleted), so I wondered if you wanted to pay it forward and share what you learned with whoever might be reading this.

CV: About six years ago when I started making music, I just had a laptop. Even today, I don't have a MIDI keyboard, so everything's just from the computer. That's just 'cos of lack of space [laughs]. So, Grimes had created this master post that was like, "This is everything you need to make music," and that's how I figured it all out. First, you need what you'd call a DAW, like Abelton or Garageband. And then you have an interface which is like the middle man between your instrument and your computer. Then you'd have your microphone and all your cables and stuff. So, I basically used that knowledge because I had no idea how to connect a microphone to a laptop before. I didn't know anything about the technical production of music. From there, I just went online and found the cheapest version of what I needed or went on eBay and found it used. I have this £100 guitar which I bought with my first paycheck when I was 17 and I still use it to this day and I haven't bought a new guitar because it's such a chunk of money, and why would I buy another one when this one still works? And if it ever got stolen, it would be easy to replace.

SS: There's probably a learning curve with songwriting that way, too.

CV: So, initially, I just had a microphone, an audio interface and a guitar and I just started recording, recording, recording, lots of little parts, just trying to get song structure right. You have to spend most of that time composing and working out the building blocks of a song. And that was so new for me because, even though I'd performed music before, like in orchestra, I'd never composed it. That part was so separate, so I was trying to piece it together, basically from scratch. The first EP I made was recorded with Garageband. For the second, I bought the basic version of Ableton.

I've just kept it really simple.

SS: I kind of wanted to talk to you about Downtown Boys a little bit because it seems like they were really important to you. It feels to me like we're in the era when everyone is listening to their own music unlike twenty years ago when it seemed like your entire friend group were listening to most of the same bands. I think if Downtown Boys had existed twenty years ago, they'd be that band that everyone was

listening to, kind of like a Bikini Kill or something like that. When I see them or hear their music, it feels the same as Bikini Kill to me—like the same level of political fervor and cultural significance, but we're in this milieu where everyone is in their corner listening to their favorite bands and there isn't one universal poster band, which is fine, it's just different. I don't know if you agree with that or not.

CV: Yeah, I do. Or it felt like there were a handful of bands that were big and a year later, it all started dissolving...

SS: Right, so I know you used to write for Downtown Boys' website fvckthemedia.com and they represent this sort of total culture of punk that we were talking about earlier in this interview, so what do they mean to you?

CV: I really love them as a band and they're cool people. How can I even explain it? I dunno, they're just cool people. They brought such a cool energy. They were *that band* five years ago. Every Downtown Boys show, you're like, "Yeah, this is good." I could watch them every night. I did an interview with them and took so many good pictures... Basically, they played DIY Space for London and another show after that and then I decided I had to travel to Italy to see them again and take more photos. I got on a flight, went to Milan, took more photos, hung out with them some more and then the next day was back to work in London. I think we share political beliefs, specifically with Joey being a part of the musician's union… We are just politically and personally aligned.

SS: What would you want a younger black punk reading this to know?

CV: In order for scenes to exist, you need space. You need a DIY space that isn't run by Live Nation or TicketMaster, you know. You need a community. I would say, if you're in London, join the Decolonise Collective that organizes Decolonise Fest because I think the people who do that are really helpful. These are the people I would trust, because I've been to the meetings and I've seen how much they care about ethics and making sure you are okay. They care about you as a black person. So that's what I'd say. Find people who are allied with you in your community. If you don't have that, start a zine because that's how you get to know people. You can find out about people's art process through interviewing them. Go to a DIY venue and try to meet people and make friends. Don't worry about people who are popular,

massive artists. Figure out how you want to participate in the community. Do you want to create a DIY venue? Do you want to fundraise? Do you want to start a mutual aid network?

SS: If you hadn't found punk, how do you think your life would be different?

CV: I probably would never have started making music. I wouldn't have been able to figure it out, really. There's not really transparency [in the mainstream world]. Punk really did snowball my life in a way I never would have expected.

BIG TAKEOVER:
ZINES AS A FREEDOM TECHNOLOGY FOR BLACK PUNKS AND OTHER MARGINALIZED GROUPS

NONFICTION

GOLDEN SUNRISE COLLIER

"Black punk, at its best, offers us the rare opportunity to nakedly pursue freedom. Black punk means creativity, resilience, an actively intersectional political awareness and engagement (or willingness to put in the work to learn), and a fundamental drive to interrogate the hegemony of dominant cultural norms, in the world and within, on every level through exploration and radical self-honesty."

THE TITLE OF THIS ESSAY DESCRIBES ZINES AS A FREEDOM technology—but what exactly do I mean by that? A freedom technology is anything that uplifts access or removes internal or external barriers to Black liberation, joy, accessibility, peace, healing, prosperity, etc., individually and collectively. As an African American, I am the descendant of master freedom technologists who created joy, artistry, and healing in the most hostile, highly surveilled, degrading, and inhumane circumstances. We still do! Our freedom technologies have looked (and look) like cakewalking and liberational movement, rock and roll, and pretty much every great "American" musical form, AAE/Black Sign Language and fugitive speechways, zoot suits, and other defiant emancipational fashion. Independent publishing has always been a salient freedom technology for Black folk here ever since David Walker's abolitionist masterpiece, *Walker's Appeal*, and zines are a fascinating continuation of that history.

I began my journey into self-publishing and zines to share information, create resources, and write about things that weren't being addressed in traditional publishing: Black folks and recovery justice, Black queer and trans history, precolonial queernesses and genders, and more. If there is something you want to say, scratch that—*need to say or share*—zines could also be a freedom technology for you. But, before we get into the how, let's consider the why: *why zines specifically?*

Firstly, zines are a low-surveillance mode of information distribution; something rare in our increasingly digital age. Ever since we were sold and brought here, Black folk in the United States have been under extreme, life-threatening surveillance, and the rise of the digital era has only made it worse. For all the good the internet does in connecting us, we don't actually own it and it is a highly surveilled, crypto-fascist, inherently anti-Black informational space.

For example, in this country, as many as 79 percent of Americans on the web worry about companies infringing their online privacy . . . and 86 percent of US citizens have attempted to somehow remove or decrease their digital footprint online.[1] The news is much more troubling for Black folks, with even artificial intelligence being spotlighted for life-altering anti-Black racism here and abroad.[2] Zines, by contrast, can be distributed hand to hand, person to person, and are not often subject to the broad and invasive searches and profiling of the digital space. By circumventing digital profiling, zines provide a low- to no-surveillance means of expressing, organizing, and celebrating ourselves.

Furthermore, zines can be really accessible and require very little technological acumen or skill, making them perfect for folks who are low or no tech. When I began making zines, I had a mostly analog workflow, cutting and pasting and then sending originals off to a local print shop for other aspects of production before finishing in-house. These days, my workflow is almost exclusively digital. However, zines can be made in a variety of ways: in small batches with no technology whatsoever (just patience and willpower), executed analog and scanned for digital distribution, designed with a fully digital workflow using expensive and complex software like Adobe Creative Suite, or published online with no hard copies at all. There is room for everyone!

One of the most salient ways that zines operate as a freedom technology for Black folks and other marginalized communities is

---

1. Nikolina Cveticanin, "Internet Privacy Statistics to Make You Wonder Who's Got Info on You," *Data Prot*, updated December 23, 2022, dataprot.net/statistics/internet-privacy-statistics/#:~:text=As%20statistics%20about%20internet%20privacy,have%20reported%20having%20such%20experiences.
2. "The program, Correctional Offender Management Profiling for Alternative Sanctions (Compas), was much more prone to mistakenly label black defendants as likely to reoffend—wrongly flagging them at almost twice the rate as white people (45% to 24%)." Stephen Buryani, "Rise of the racist robots—how AI is learning all our worst impulses, *The Guardian*, August 8, 2017, www.theguardian.com/inequality/2017/aug/08/rise-of-the-racist-robots-how-ai-is-learning-all-our-worst-impulses.

that they provide a space to speak authentically to our dreams and concerns, circumventing traditional publishing pathways that often tokenize and exclude Black folks (or accept such an extremely narrow topical range beholden to shallow capitalistic notions of Blackness and profitability that it is almost entirely inaccessible). As Tracy Sherrod, editorial director at Amistad, points out, "Sometimes there are proposals that come along, and you know in your heart that this is an important book on an important subject, but because the editorial room is all white, you may not be able to acquire it, so the only really painful thing about racism in publishing is the books that are not around, the books that didn't get to be published."[3] A powerful desire for more editorial control sent many of our legendary artists into the publishing world. For example, Toni Morrison's advocacy as editor at Random House is the singular reason the work of Gayl Jones, Toni Cade Bambara, Henry Dumas, and Angela Davis's biography were published. Zines put you in the driver's seat and offer *anyone* a chance to speak from the source. Also, unlike publishing work through major publishing houses, zines allow for creativity and flexibility of distribution that is 100 percent creator controlled. You (or your collective, community group, class, etc.) can control every aspect of their design, format, content, materials, editing, etc.

Zines are also an all-ages tool, which makes them perfect for another highly surveilled population—children and teens! Youth are stripped of most civic powers and autonomy in this country, but zines are a way for them to organize, speak their minds, and distribute their thinking beyond the control of adults who are not their accomplices. Youth and children's communications (especially radical communication that rightfully questions the legitimacy of adult hegemony and authority) is often shut down by adults or dismissed

---

3. "'A Conflicted Cultural Force': What It's Like to Be Black in Publishing," interviews by Concepción de León, Alexandra Alter, Elizabeth A. Harris, and Joumana Khatib, *The New York Times*, July 1, 2020, www.nytimes.com/2020/07/01/books/book-publishing -black.html.

as trivial, but children and youth are critical voices that have always contributed so much imagination, innovation, and vitality to every aspect of civic life. Kids deserve to be heard on their own terms. What other groups deserve the mic?

Zines are a part of a long and rugged history of independent small presses bringing forth works that were deemed unworthy by major publishing houses. Small presses like Kitchen Table Press and the Crossing Press took a chance and published Black feminist classics such as *All the Women Are White, All the Blacks Are Men, but Some of Us Are Brave* and Audre Lorde's seminal *Sister Outsider*. It was a small press that published W. E. B. Du Bois's *The Souls of Black Folk* in 1903, twelve years before D. W. Griffith's Klan fanboy film *Birth of a Nation* and *fifty-two years* before Black women seized the right to vote!

For African Americans in particular: We have been excluded from literate life for most of the history of the United States despite our undeniable cultural and scientific contributions to every aspect of national life. We were legally forbidden from learning to read and touching or owning books. It was a capital offense to *teach* us to read or recognize the alphabet. *We know more than most* the fugitivity inherent to Black literacy, as evidenced further by our creation of public schools during reconstruction. *We understand more than most* the importance of reading and protecting the dissemination of radical ideas that are free from surveillance.

Fast-forward to the late twentieth century and beyond, and Black punks have carried the torch forward in high style! For punks in general, the affordability, anti-authoritarian, low-surveillance aspects of this form align closely with the overall ethos. While punk, like so many subcultures under capitalism, has been deeply co-opted, punk zine subculture is still very much alive, and Black punks and creatives continue to utilize this publishing form to speak authentically and directly.

Some of the Black zinesters whose work I admire and appreciate include: Cassandra Press, The Tenth, Gal-Dem, Laneha House, Ulterior Zines, FIYAH! LitMag, Shotgun Seamstress, and Blk Grl's Wurld, to name a few.

Badass Historical Black zines I discovered in my research over the years include: W.E.B. Dubois' The Brownies Book (a children's periodical from the early twentieth century) and FIRE! (a Harlem renaissance superstar periodical featuring work by Zora, Langston, etc)– we been out cherel

So, without further ado, I'm going to walk you through three ways to freak an analog classic zine form: the one-pager! One-pagers are timeless and versatile because they are easy to make and affordable to assemble, produce, and distribute. They can be made quickly and without fancy or complex materials, perfect for feisty beginners or seasoned pros with something to say. Organization is key with the last two formats. Other than that, all you need is one page and your imagination!

Level 1: The Electric Slide

This is the classic one-page design that provides users with eight pages of text space (minus two pages for the front and back covers).

Pros: Quick and easy with only a few pages to fill up. No cutting required! Simple layout. Can be taken to print shops as-is for production.

Cons: Leaves lots of blank space on unused sides. Not the best for one-pagers that need more space. Can't be leveraged up into a multi-one-page format. Pages are a bit tiny.

fold yr paper
in half

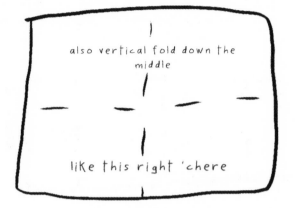

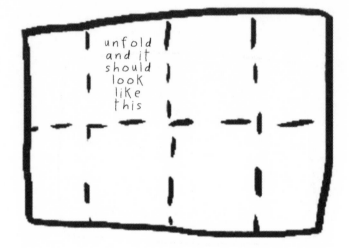

unfold
and it
should
look
like
this

stop

fold the paper
halfway and
cut to the
first vertical
fold (and NO
further)

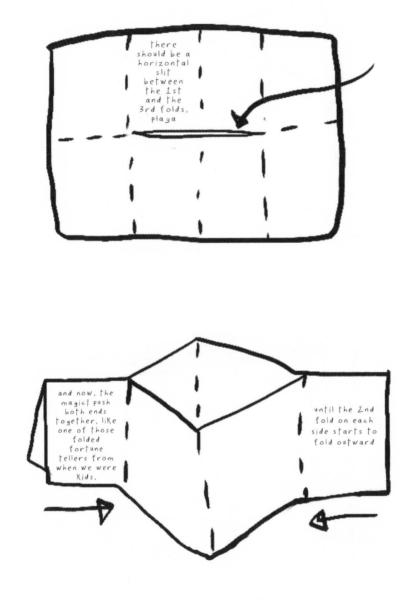

there should be a horizontal slit between the 1st and the 3rd folds, playa

and now, the magic! push both ends together, like one of those folded fortune tellers from when we were kids.

until the 2nd fold on each side starts to fold outward

fold up your new zine and

freak nasty: the space opera

Bim! Your new 8 page zine is ready to take the world by storm! Just unfold and take to your local copy shop!

Level 2: The Cupid Shuffle

This is the one-page format I designed when I started wanting more space. This form provides two pages for text and artwork (and front and back cover) but can easily be adjusted to include as many pages as your long-arm stapler will allow.

Pros: Can easily be leveraged up to contain more pages. Pages are 4¼" by 5½" and can have a portrait or landscape orientation. No wasted space.

Cons: Flimsy as a one-pager (best if multiple sheets of paper). Complex layout, cutting required.

this one starts a lot like the last.
create a horizontal fold
(dealer's choice- use either landscape or portrait
as long as you stick with it!)

fold in half again so
that you now have a
cross shaped fold

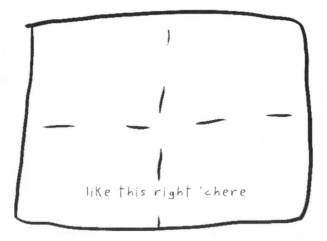

like this right 'chere

this one page design offers
bigger page sizes and an
easier folding & cutting scheme.

I will lay out what a two-sheet
version would look like, but
you can just keep adding more pages
(I've done up to 4 sheets before which =
32 pages total in the finished zine,
but higher than that could be too hard
to staple - try and lmk!)

front of sheet 1

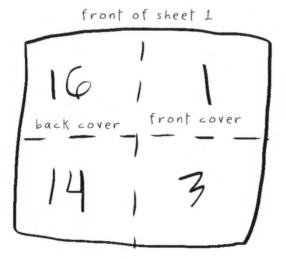

inside of sheet 1

front of sheet two

inside of sheet two

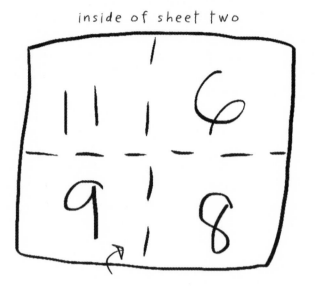

These two pages, 8 & 9, will be
facing each other so consider
this centerfold when you are
designing! Once all your pages
are designed, the last step would
be to take the pages to your
local printer for replication and
then a final cut across the
whole stack with their cutter
(most big box printers have
hydraulic cutters than can cut
hundreds of sheets at a time)!
Then you can assemble and
distribute! ♡

Level 3: The Wobble

This one-page design produces standard-size zines. I used this format as my default analog workflow when I first started out. This format offers pages that are 5½ by 8½ inches.

Pros: Can be taken to printers as is. No cutting required. No wasted space.

Cons: Depending on how many pages you use, this format can become somewhat unwieldy. Document management and organization of originals is crucial.

other considerations:

* the sheets can be any size. You could, for example, make a one page zine out of an 11x17 in. sheet!

*if you're not sending this off to a printer (ex. making a bday zine for a friend), you can use any kind of paper you want— get creative!

*Once you've got at least one of two zines, then you can start applying for fests! Fests are a great way to see possibilities and link with other zinesters.

*most copy shops cannot accommodate designs with full bleeds (color that runs right up to the edge with no margin), so plan for margins accordingly! however, if you scan the orginals in and format them digitally, a great place for printing is Fireball Printing in Philly, which prints full bleeds beautifully.

Fold your paper in half. Most folks choose to fold down the middle with a landscape orientation, but if you're feeling frisky, you can always switch it up and fold with a portrait orientation for a tall book!

Once you've completed the fold, you've gotten through the most difficult part (congrats!) No cutting required, just design and take to the printers!

Each single sheet will produce 4 pages with this basic design.

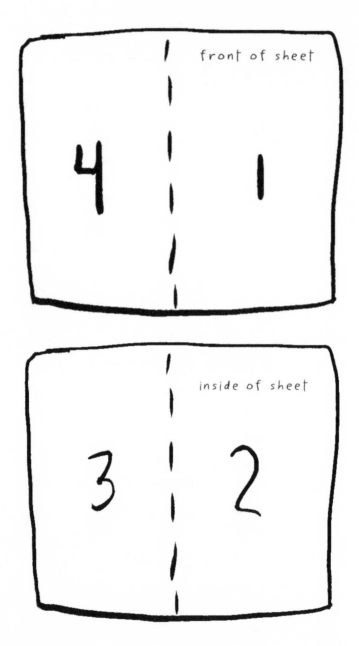

We need your words, your artwork, and your voice! Zines are a freedom technology that liberate us from needing anyone's permission to express what is on our minds, and if you make a zine, I'd love to see it and digitally high-five ya.

In closing, I will leave you with this bit of game from one of our patron saints of giving no fucks, Audre Lorde: "What are the words you do not yet have? What do you need to say? What are the tyrannies you swallow day by day and attempt to make your own, until you will sicken and die of them, still in silence?" What brilliance will you use this freedom technology to unleash, friends?

Regardless, good luck out there. I'm rooting for you, and happy zine-ing!

yr pal always,

golden

OPT OUT:
RECLAIMING DIGITAL PRIVACY IN AN OMNISCIENT ERA

NONFICTION

A CONVERSATION WITH MATT MITCHELL

INTERVIEW BY ASHAKI M. JACKSON

MATT MITCHELL JOINS OUR VIRTUAL CALL IN FULL COLOR, CRISP in his long sleeves and suit vest. Micro-twists crown his fade. His eyes are bright and calm despite the recent Independence Day fireworks that, over the pandemic years, have felt increasingly powerful enough to split the ground. Matt is dressed to be seen—a type of courage for a hacker in New York City.

Prior to our conversation, I read up on his history, laugh at the comedic timing during his cameo on *Full Frontal with Samantha Bee,* and sort through a short Google image library of his stylish images. Matt Mitchell is online. It feels counterintuitive for a Black man to be purposely visible in light of his work as founder of CryptoHarlem, a nonprofit that helps educate the masses on securities against surveillance and autonomy from technological spies. Mutual friend Chris L. Terry describes Matt's work as "hacking for liberation"—an act of resistance and preservation familiar to their punk youth—and had been eager to introduce us based on our shared interest in surveillance.

Motivated by the media treatment of Michael Brown's death, I have spent the past several years exploring surveillance through creative writing and codework, including the public's role in scrutinizing Black people. The public is often keen to serve as witness and jury when watching widely available videos of police killing Black civilians. The presumption that Black people are inherently immoral or external to America's design—thus deserving of being watched closely—is a tenet of how this nation functions. Cameras sprouting from lamp posts, home security systems, Cambridge Analytica, and Amazon's Alexa are surrogates, allowing the net of who is watched to be cast much wider and the watchers to be further obscured.

My studies have yielded a few academics who are deeply engaged in revealing the pervasiveness of surveillance off- and online, but Matt is the first hacker or security researcher. He and I reserve an hour to talk about where our knowledge of surveillance collides. Despite several minutes of being foiled by video conferencing software, we settle on a program that optimizes our ability to see and hear each other on opposite coasts. Staring in the general area of our computer cameras, we agree to become subjects of the discussion topic and press record.

—Ashaki M. Jackson

THE CORNER PREACHER

AJ: Why CryptoHarlem?

MM: I was looking for a job when I was younger. I think I was twenty-one. I went to this temp agency to be like, "Hey, I'm a computer person. You have any computer jobs?" And they wanted me to take this computer test. (This is, man, a long time ago.) They came back to me and said, "You're off the charts. We've never seen anything like this before. Hey, listen, there's this client . . . Could you take this special test that we set up for them?" And I took that test. "We need you to just start at this place." So, I just went, and it was good money. Little did I know.

A month in, my managers called me in. I thought I did something wrong, and they're like, "No, no, you're great here. We want to tell you about what your real job is." My real job? "We've been watching you. We just set up this job for a reason, trying to find the right people to be on this team to do the real job."

What's the real job? "You need to watch everyone who works here. We need you to surveil and let us know what everyone who works here is dealing with, writing, thinking, with their email and everything."

And I was like, Yo, is that legal? "They sign employee agreements. But, especially the folks with the foreign passports. Double-scan them, you know?" And I was like, Damn. That's when I was introduced to the world of corporate surveillance.

AJ: My heart is jumping. It's shaking. It's angry. (Laughter)

MM: Yeah, it's horrible, right? I'm not even from here. I'm an immigrant. My parents are immigrants and foreign passport holders. I spent the whole month talking to people, being all friendly, now I gotta be like a super snitch? It's wild. How much do I need this job?

I tried to leave that job. I changed my resume around. But, the same thing happened. This time, it was two weeks in.

AJ: Oh my gosh, you've been marked!

MM: So there was something about my resume that said I'm a bloodhound. I'm a people hunter. And it really bothered me, especially as a punk, as an activist, and somebody who's really trying to change the system and shatter the status quo. This is against the ethos that I believe in.

I was working a job at *The New York Times* as a data journalist. It was the beginning of all the years of extrajudicial killing of Black men in this country. I needed to do something. Everyone's like, Yo, that's messed up, man. That's my average employee interaction. But to the Black folks at work, it was like a family member died. It's all that childhood trauma but with death attached, one after another. And that could have been me, that could have been my cousin, my sister, my brother. Listen, I needed to do something. So, I started CryptoHarlem. I was living in Harlem. I went to community centers, churches, a mosque just trying to find a place to work and talk to people. And there was this one on the corner of Malcolm X and Martin Luther King, I kid you not. Doesn't get any better.

Harlem Business Alliance, props to them, they let me do my first event. I would love to tell you there was just one person there, and we just grew it from there. But no, it was packed! People were just like, looking in from the street. It was packed because I was selling a remedy to a pain that everybody has.

And I was explaining like, See that street pole right there? This is what that thing is, this is how it works, and this is how you can avoid it. You know those lights blasting into your windows in the projects? This is who put that there, this is how it's funded, how it's powered, and this is the gain. It's empowering. We're Black folks. We know, our grandmammas know, their grandmammas knew that we're being watched. Now it's really just me telling folks which things they were always right on. And which things they were like, just a little off. Like discussing 5G in the [Black] barbershop. I'm like, I don't know, bro, if it really causes COVID. (Laughter) But every airport has no 5G near it because the FAA and the FCC are thinking over whether it can down planes. And that is a problem. And here's how that problem started.

Why CryptoHarlem? Because I love Black people. And if we can stop this stuff now—the multi-levels of surveillance that happen in any Black community, we have a chance. If we can stop it in the hood, which is the Petri dish, the beta test lab—then we have a chance. But by the time it hits the dominant culture in the suburbs, it will be strong and unstoppable. It'll be a tank. But by the time they're like, "This is wrong," it's too late, fam.

We get recognition from all people because this is everybody's fight. It takes all of us to stop these robots right here. If we can't, if we lose this ground (this is sacred ground), we lose the hood, we lose the countryside. We lose where the Black and Brown people stand, people of color stand, undocumented folks stand, sex workers stand, queer folks stand, trans folks stand. If we lose that ground to the robots, then we'll lose it all. We're not just people who can tell you "This is bad" or that we can push back and advocate. We're hackers. We teach folks that if you want to find bias in code, you gotta learn how to write, read code. So, we're going to teach you how to read Python. Or, you gotta get certified in cybersecurity so you can understand. It requires you to get skilled up, but those skills also help you make money. It's a good thing for everybody.

It's not an accident that your average person who knows and does this stuff isn't a Black person. At the same time, the people who are fighting for all our rights are Black folks because they're directly impacted. I really believe directly impacted people will solve our problems. We didn't need the opportunity, but the knowledge, and the knowledge part is hard.

People have babies, people got bills to pay. Our condition is not by accident. Those conditions are not conducive to learning cybersecurity. I don't want to reach that W. E. B. Du Bois of the hood, I want to reach that person with a tattoo on their neck and they're on their fifth job and third kid, and they are realizing that things are stacked against them for no reason. I want to give them this new profession where there's more jobs than people. Employers are too desperate to hire to be racist. You could be like, "I don't have a GED," and they're like, "But you have the cybersecurity skills. Let's go."

I see this opportunity for us as a people. And we need those folks to win when the robots come anyway.

NEIGHBORS

AJ: My landlord set up cameras around the building. You can see them. He did not ask permission. And it just threw the neighborhood in a tizzy because we didn't have cameras until white people started to move in. So, there's this invasiveness. When you talk about tearing down someone with these surveillance tools, we experienced that here. We used to look out for each other, and that was in our possession. Whether it's coming outside and saying hi, and looking after the neighborhood kids while they're on their bikes, or we could be peeking through the curtains because we're nosy. But that's what we would do. Then, somebody else from outside the neighborhood put cameras there, and we all agreed: violation. What is this doing here? We can see it watching us. And that feels demeaning, disrespectful, etc. Do you take them down? Of course not.

At the start of this conversation, you and I were on a platform called Wire. That was a new platform to me, and it had great, basic security features, including scheduling your chat messages to disappear. You're very much in the game of protecting information. We know what it is to be surveilled on the outside. What does it mean to be online in this age of surveillance? Does online mean that I'm just turning on my computer and logging into social media? Where is surveillance reaching me online?

MM: When you go online, you're told it's like jumping in a car and getting on the information superhighway, moving toward something. That's not how it works. The minute you're attached to the internet, you're given a serial number that is connected to your location on the planet Earth. It's a door you're opening the minute you're connected.

They need to know where you are, who you are, and what you are before they can monetize you. They need to know that you're Black, a woman, in a metropolitan area, and they want to monetize to the highest level. Before we do anything, that's happened to us. IP address, neighborhood, ZIP code, and you paid for this package, and because of your name we think you're probably worth X amount, so they're gonna show you this ad for health insurance or a car and it's mad, mad, expensive, compared to if you were in another part of town. That's real. The way that it works is so invisible. Your internet is not my internet, and our internet is not the internet of someone who lives in a different place or has different racial identity. You can't have agency until you can have control over that.

We're surveilled the minute we pay for internet access. The minute your device is touched, the system is already trying to size you up and squeeze you to get pennies, dimes, dollars.

All these companies have a front door to law enforcement as a courtesy, not because they legally have to. Facebook.com/Records is a front door for law enforcement. LERS.Google.com. That's a front door for law enforcement. Everyone has one. And law enforcement uses tools to aggregate huge amounts of data. They're looking and hunting for us as Black folks. Because of your social media posts, the picture you put up, the video you made, a song you wrote, a text you wrote, you're now criminalized and law enforcement is looking for you. That's another danger for us. We do what they told us to do—express yourself, put up your pictures, share with your friends—but we don't get treated the same as other users.

AJ: I'm thinking about Professor Simone Browne's book *Dark Matters* within which she was describing some technology that doesn't pick up darker skin tones, or creates ghosts of us in some earlier versions of equipment like cameras.

I wonder what your thoughts are on surveillance misidentifying us? One, you shouldn't have our information; two, you have our information and you misidentify us; and three, this is all part of a system to criminalize us. How do we reclaim our identities, if it's possible?

MM: Yeah, it's 100 percent possible. I'm not Mr. Doom and Gloom. I'm Mr. Hope, and I love technology. I'm a big tech nerd. I'm a software engineer. I'm a computer hacker. When I first tell Black folks facial recognition systems have a problem with us, they're like Cool! Now we're ghosts; we can do whatever we want. No. What it means is now, the dragnet pulls us all in, and we're all on the lineup together. It happens so frequently, where people get misidentified by computers for crimes, and it's just the lucky ones who don't get charged with any crime. It becomes a story in *The New York Times*, or *The New Yorker*, or the ACLU picks up the case. But those are just the perfect stories.

Rosa Parks was a perfect story. She worked for the NAACP, she was very fair-skinned, super smart, and she knew there was a problem with busing and segregation. But, she's not the first person to be like, Nah, I'm not getting up. Not by far. But we needed a perfect story, so we could galvanize a community around a secretary who is super chill and conservative. But, you look at Claudette Colvin, who was pregnant out of wedlock, dark-skinned, and young. No, I'm tired. I'm not going to move my seat. Nobody came to support her because she wasn't a perfect story.

There was this case in New Jersey. This person supposedly drove into a police car and then escaped. The police misidentify this brotha, but he was nowhere near the scene of the crime. The facial recognition system told the cops to go talk to him. Any Black person would have been like, These two brothas don't look anything alike at all.

Brotha lived really far away. He was a youth basketball coach. He was the perfect story. Even though he got caught up in this spider web, he got out of it because of all these lucky breaks. That's not always what happens. Maybe you're not doing what you should be doing; you're just trying to do what you feel is right, you're living by your own moral code, and it's not so perfect. Then they don't write about you. Then the system shouldn't have picked you, but you were bad anyway. And nobody really is championing your cause. But, I champion your cause . . .

When it comes to these things, how do we protect ourselves? One is we need to know all our stories, not just the perfect ones. When you read one of those perfect ones, there's probably ten imperfect ones behind them. Find their stories. Look out for them.

WATCHING AS WARFARE

AJ: As a social psychologist, I've been thinking about perspective and Heider's theory of perception. We look at something and make decisions about what we are seeing based on the environment, like lighting (if we're able to see things clearly); what we understand the world to be and how we think people should be acting; how we're feeling that day; if we are focused (are we paying attention?); if we think these events are static; was it the actor's fault, or was it the environment for what we just saw? I said to myself, I must be missing something that Heider didn't add. Some piece in this conversation about the way that Americans—United Statesians—look at Black people.

The work that I'm doing now is a poetry manuscript called *Convergence*. Convergence is the way your eyesight clears up when something approaches you. And convergence insufficiency happens when something approaches you, but your sight remains blurred. It reminds me of a person seeing a Black man walking toward them during daylight, and maybe they have their glasses on, versus a Black man walking toward them at night, and they don't have their glasses on. That is the perception that we are working with—the perpetual misunderstanding of who or what is approaching. Then there's also what we think we know in terms of how people behave. The structure that we are trying to escape is, how does the nation understand Black people in terms of behavior (what they expect us to do)? When they perceive us, it's never going to be clear, and it's never going to be in our favor. White gaze—that's what I'm trying to work through in my poetry and some of the codework that I've been exploring.

Let's talk about surveillance systems. Is this security? Is this white gaze? Both?

MM: The difference between us and a lot of the other animals we share this planet with is that we can think up new tool development. There's all these studies about how some birds use sticks. In an experiment, researchers modified things so the bird could only reach food with a stick. The bird bent it into a tool to get the food. Animals develop tools.

Surveillance systems are a huge leap in tool development. We don't just make tools for catching food. We make tools for killing and hurting other human beings, and surveillance is one of those weapons. That's what it always has been. When we talk about slave ships and property, and keeping track of that property, that's surveillance. When we talk about overseers on a plantation monitoring human beings like they're chattel, that's surveillance too. When we have groups of people looking for runaway slaves, and wanted posters, that's surveillance.

Surveillance is an interesting weapon because it allows you to other the target in such a way that you strip them of their humanity, which is necessary, because it is a thing that you use when you don't have (someone's) trust.

It is a weapon that targets all marginalized communities, but especially Black folks. It's part of our story, and it's always been part of our story. While our conditions have changed, and our generations have changed, this weapon is always used on us. But, it's different in what it looks like.

An interesting thing about the modern technology of surveillance is that the weapon is invisible now. It used to be you could see the overseer, you could see the guard in the prison tower. Now, it's debatable whether it exists. One of the hardest parts of my job is explaining that we are under fire by this weapon, because you can't see it.

I talk about it as digital stop-and-frisk. They never got rid of it.

Every cop needs to get a certain number of stops. Black people, children, our elders—the people who hold the wisdom—can be and are just thrown up against the wall. [Officers] violate your space, dump your stuff on the ground, stick their fingers inside of you, whatever they got to do to just get some stops and hopefully find something.

Now, you could be at work, just living your best life, but digitally, that's happening to all your data and your identity. It's maybe even being criminalized and may lead to you being indicted. You have no way to tell what's happening to the virtual version of you. It's being thrown up against the wall while you're hanging out in the break room.

That's my life's work—helping us as a people see this dangerous, harmful, invisible force, and to take actions to immediately protect ourselves, or at least circumvent some of the surveillance.

GOING DARK

MM: I make this joke about Google Maps, when it's telling me what neighborhood to walk through, it's trying to get me killed! (Laughter)

Probably would be a *Green Book*–type situation; when you're taking a trip, you wouldn't just listen to the data and do what it tells you to do. You'd be like, "That's not for me. I'm not gonna fall for that." You'd ask, "Are there other people who look like me there?" And if there weren't, you might code-switch for your safety. And you might feel, "I need to be not as myself right now. I need to be really cautious right now, just in case."

Well, that's how technology use needs to be for us. Just how you already do the inconvenient stuff for your safety in the real world, in the digital world you've got to take a little five minutes and just go in and turn the data faucet off. Go in and change those settings.

Personalization means systems figuring out what I am, who I am to the highest level possible. So, turn off personalization; it's usually under Advertising or Privacy.

In any app you use, try to use the website version, not the mobile phone version because that gets access to other parts of your device.

Your phone is actually a box filled with sensors. The webpage can only get basic web information—what you put into it. When you're laying down looking at Facebook, the phone knows you're laying down. They collect huge amounts in the app but in the browser they can't. Go into personalization, turn that off. Go into Privacy settings, read it, and uncheck stuff.

If you go to MyActivity.Google.com, it's everything Google has on you. I tell people the first thing you want to do is pause everything. You can see every YouTube video you've ever looked at in the order you looked at it. Delete it wholesale. Every search you've ever written: lymph node swollen, throat dry, am I sick, WebMD told you that you died three months ago. (Laughter) It's all in there. Just delete it. It will ask you, "Are you sure? This might affect the quality of your . . ." Just delete it.

You can go to maps.google.com/locationhistory, and it might show you everywhere you've ever been. Nobody needs to know that. They give us the controls to delete, but they don't want us to delete. Everything's on by default, sending it to somebody you shouldn't be sending it to by default. Take the ten minutes.

NO WHITES ON THE MIC

ROUNDTABLE

HOW DID YOU GET INTO PUNK

HOW DO Y'ALL TEND TO SELF-CARE?

How did you get into punk?

MONIKA

I initially got into punk in my teens, growing up in Milwaukee, Wisconsin. Around that time, I was an active member on the Afro-Punk message boards. That's initially what got me into the scene. Then, when I was twentysomething, I moved to Chicago and encountered the punk scene there. Going to Chicago was an eye opener for me because there's a huge Latinx punk scene, like with Los Crudos and all those other bands.

STEPHANIE

I first got into punk when I was a teenager, kind of vicariously through listening to lots of indie—there was lots of British indie bands which had people of color members, like Bloc Party.

I very slowly got more and more into punk because I found out about Riot Grrrl. I was listening to Bikini Kill and Bratmobile. Getting that element of politics through music and seeing how they can be combined was really integral for me. It taught me you can create your own culture instead of just consuming it. And when I figured out I wanted to be a journalist, I started my own music blog, writing about women in punk. I got involved in a festival called Ladyfest 10, which is about bringing more women and female-fronted bands to stages. And then eventually started my own band.

SHANNA

I got into punk probably around 2015. I was going to a lot of anarchist spaces, a lot of communist spaces. We were really talking about Black radicalism, anti-police organizing, and turns out a lot of people in those spaces are also punk too. So I met a lot of really cool Black anarchists, who were directing me to punk spaces in Chicago.

At that time, I was looking for a wider, broader community who understood my political values. So I figured that the punk scene was probably the best place to be around people like that—to learn, to grow from, and to organize with. I went to a show on the Southside of Chicago and I immediately fell in love with it. It felt really liberating.

As you're organizing, how do y'all tend to your self-care?

SHAWNA

I'm very into bubble-bath bath products and massages. I loved living in Oakland and San Francisco because they have the Korean spas. I love the beach. You know, just taking that time off and being in a space that I enjoy.

Also, something I had to learn is lying the fuck down. Self-care doesn't have to be doing stuff, just lie the fuck down.

CHRISTINA

Previously, I was running programs at *The New York Times*. And I've found over the years that there's a whole lot more stress in my life navigating those spaces. So I turn to #Blkgrlswurld, a project where we have full control to come up with new ideas. Let me just go do something with my hands where I'm not using my mind at all, to alleviate stress from the day job.

I've always had a mission for #Blkgrlswurld: it's supposed to be fun. If it starts to feel like work, then it's going down the wrong path for us.

SCOUT

[After the fest] I just had to get out of town for like four days. I didn't know how important it was until the second year. I was like "I gotta get out" and my partner took me to the beach and it was amazing. So definitely taking care of yourself.

Therapy, if you can get it.

WHAT I SAY

NONFICTION

KYLE OZERO

AS TOLD TO JAMES SPOONER

"Reactions were instantaneous. I was told that I was 'marked.' I was told that I should be 'made' to shut up. Whenever someone posts it up, it starts all over again. I assume it'll be like this for years to come."

WHEN PEOPLE GOOGLE ICONIC ROCK 'N' ROLL IMAGES, I WANT them to be reminded of the truth.

The response is typically negative, ranging from death threats to memes. It's a steady stream of hate.

Despite acts getting signed and playing fests, these comments are a good gauge of where Black people stand in rock 'n' roll. We are not included in the greater conversation of rock 'n' roll's legacy acts, but we need to be.

Rock 'n' roll is Black music and we won't be erased.

Photograph by Audrey Arrington

Photograph by Emilou

Photograph by Emilou

Photograph by Jim Blissitt III

Johnny Ramone
was
a

RACIST

Are you a racist too?

Rock N' Roll has always been black music.

Photograph by Emilou

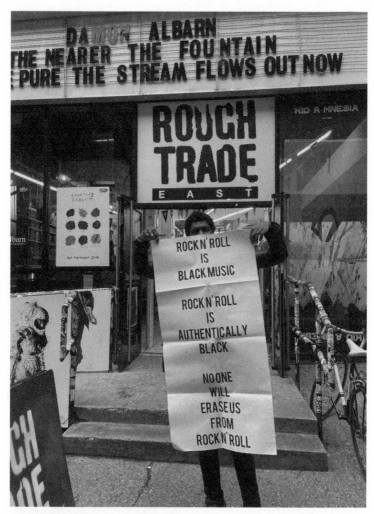

Photograph by Emilou

SMOKE AGAIN, AKHI

FICTION

ALEX SMITH

I think Rancid was my first [s]how, although it didn't really [a]ffect me. My first DIY show how[e]ver? Different story. July 4, [1]994 at the Dick Street House in [G]reenboro, NC. Policy of 3, Shot[m]aker, Propagandhi, FYP, Quincy [P]unx. My first time experiencing [t]he culture in such a visceral [w]ay—zines, riot grrls, queer [p]unks, food not bombs, hand[m]ade record sleeves, bands [s]creaming their head off in [s]omeone's living room— [t]hat show changed [m]y worldview."

J. Spooner 22

PART I

NYX—SWIRLING BITS OF LIVING IRON AND ONYX, LIKE STRANGE gateways—and Kentavious still cried when he heard someone say they looked like new adinkra. They were fleshy, smoky shadows stretching out their hands and fading into the sky that held them, sinking into the seams of night fabric, illuminated only by a star or two that got stuck in orbit over the 'hood. Like black crescent clouds, machines appeared in the Philadelphia skyline. Orotund discs that just pushed through the cement, uprooting trees and wrapping their veined limbs into form.

In the days following, neon provided more light, more comfort—a Chinese store was a blinding oasis where Newport boxes and a glass plate protected the faces of candy and crunch bars, of snack cakes, bathed in fluorescence.

"Loud out," one of them boys called, so subtly under his breath, so smoky and wet the words were in his throat. It was a familiar sound, a voice with a husk created by Rap Chips and Jungle Juice—a shy thuggish timbre wrought with ash. It was night, but children played in and out of the doors. Women chastised them; an older man shook his head, then reached into his long, brown suede trench coat, ran his bony fingers through his five-o'clock shadow, and then tapped on the glass in an impatient huff.

"Five, ten minutes," the small woman behind the glass called, a rehearsed response rushed and clear, plain. The older man sighed again, then under his breath reminded her, "That's what you said about five, ten minutes ago."

Kentavious looked around the small expanse of the green-tiled vestibule, where the stench of burning meat hovered cloud-thick. He instinctively sniffed at his own clothes.

"What? You ain't smoking?" the loud man asked. His eyes were amber marbles dim and foggy in their sockets, pushed behind a stout, chubby face and hidden by a dense, uncontrolled mane. The dingy white T-shirt he wore draped over the plump curves of his body, a shirt the slight sheen of which revealed sheets of dark flesh underneath. His thick fingers pinched at a tiny rolled cigarette that looked like a single star nearly smothered in the vast expanse of his hands. Kentavious absorbed him in seconds—the aroma like nag champa and bacon, the softness purpling around his lips, the thighs like two mastiffs in his lap covered in loose-fitting jeans, and the buttery, scuff-free mustard Timbs hugging tightly to his enormous feet— Kentavious didn't like to check men out, he liked to ingest them, to suffocate on their wholeness, to dream about them as he passed them. He found this type of thrilling guerilla assessment impossible to do at clubs or raves or gay bookstores, on the apps or even in cruising parks where a kind of elegiac danger wafted in the air and mingled with the smell of leather and bourbon and semen—in these spaces men were too open, there was no ambiance, just the sheer force of themselves splayed out to disco beats, all mystery danced away under the raw strobe lights.

"Yes, you called? Tofu! You had tofu!" the woman behind the counter exclaimed. "Tofu and bean sprouts, yes?" At that moment, of course, she chose professionalism, promptness, and a perfection in calling out his order, a colloquial approach that felt homely instead of the usual coldness. He pushed past the older man who grew grumpier, now looking at his phone surely cursing the fact that he didn't call ahead. The swirl of danger around him as older kids, then teenagers, then men appeared in and out of the store, sometimes backlit in the blue light of a police car, their laughter thorned with sadness and desperation. Kentavious could see it in their toothy smiles, their black gums, their off-white eyes.

He handed the woman money through a small hole in the glass, then reached around a nook in the glass wall and grabbed his food, eyes fixed on the floor between him and the loud man and said, "Nah, I'm good."

Just outside, the air had cooled significantly. A slight breeze grew into a bit of wind as it kicked up plastic grocery bags and gum wrappers and dead leaves. The young men by the door stopped, slowly climbed off of their bikes, and did something they rarely ever did until recently—they looked up. The loud man shuffled his large frame through the doorway and stood beside Kentavious, his leathery scent even stronger outside the restaurant where it didn't have to compete with french fries and wontons. The older man stormed out, his food finally in tow, barking into his phone, "Yeah, no, I forgot you had said you had wanted fried rice, Sheila. I'm not going back in there, I—" The older man looked at his phone. It was suddenly dead. All around them was silent and still; a police car in front of the store parked diagonally across lanes, the officers out of their vehicles and hats in their hands. "Jesus Christ," the old man said under his breath as wind swept at his collar, light crackled in front of them, and a large circle of metallic, black fibers hovered in the sky, abuzz with light and smelling of ozone.

"These things are real?" the older man said, turning to Kentavious and the loud man. "I—I didn't think they were real," he said, a tremor in his voice. He turned a pale, ashy brown under the neon light.

The wind died down and the circle dissolved. What was left were fibrous ash that sparked around the sky like embers. The older man walked away, got into his SUV, and left. Others dispersed. "You sure you don't want that hook up?" loud man asked Kentavious, not looking at him but out into the street.

Kentavious smiled. He reflexively, nervously glanced at his phone and opened Scruff. A faster, further cry were the apps; each time he read a guy yet felt still a desperate, instinctive pull toward him, Kentavious opened an app. He looked at his viewers first; same as seven hours ago, none of them interesting. The closest to him was a profile with no picture. He clicked on it. The profile was blank save for the gray, shadowy avatar the app defaults to and the word-phrase "sup?" <1,500 feet.

Kentavious looked up from his phone and reflexively stared at the beautiful man who was trying to sell him really bad drugs. A wave of kinetic energy coursed through him like The Force but on crack.

Besides, there was too much encroaching white dick on that app—a "bunch of gaycist cis boys with arrested development issues," his friend Cici called them; so he put his phone away. But they were moving into the 'hood, he thought—white gay men, with their flood of feigned affluence, hot on the heels of the artists and the activists. Soon they would start renting the apartments above the Chinese restaurants and bodegas and liquor stores, rent prices would go up, and the already suffocating police presence would increase. He'd have to say hi to them, have to stop playing bongos with the old head dreads out in front of his cousin's barbershop for fear of one of the new citizenry calling in a noise complaint. Kentavious would look up one day, he thought, and see the fish fry place he used to get amazing sides from gone. He'd wonder, staring at a paint stain on his Uniqlo joggers and suede Clyde Fraziers, his hands tucked into his puffy Members Only bomber jacket, if he hadn't paved the way that led them here.

"Nah, I can't fuck with that right now. I just got out," Kentavious answered. It sounded tougher than it was; somehow he knew it would impress. He had just gotten out of jail, sure, but for being one too many a Black body crossing police lines at a protest for a Black man killed by an off-duty cop. He'd slipped past the wall of white students that would casually form at these things and he'd been stuck on the fringe, his camera in hand to document it, and got caught with a baton. He hit the ground hard, raised his hands instinctively to protect himself, when several riot cops came in swinging, bruising his ulna. The last thing he remembered was seeing Marissa's perky, white face, draped in fading blue hair, yelling in his face, something like, "Don't worry, the fund will cover you! We'll get you free, Kent!" A small chorus of "Free Kent!" bubbled up around his ears, his vision went hazy, then black, and he awoke on a hospital gurney, handcuffed to the bed's railing.

Two men that had been in and out of the store were hugging in the street. A slow, nervous warmth crept over Kentavious. "Damn, you did a bid?" Kentavious nodded gently. The two men watched the other two men hug, their pants sagging below their waists, their wife beaters pocked with sweat stains, their cornrows and baby-dreads tucked one under a beanie, the other under a Phillies cap. They watched the children start the slow walk home with a sheen to their eyes. They watched lightning bugs dance.

"—name John."

"Kentavious."

John's momma's house was around the corner. Kentavious sat on a rusting IKEA chair's edge, leaning over the kitchen table, his eyes darting around like mice in a maze as he glanced at the objects placed there. Magazines, crossword puzzles, and instruction manuals from Xbox games sat in a pile next to an ashtray, three empty glasses perfect for bourbon, and a gun.

"Gon' head and finish eating, then we can light this shit." John pulled bags of weed out of his pants. He put them on the table in front of Kentavious, lifted the nub of a cigarette to his lips, and pulled slowly on it, increasing his inhalation until the cigarette nearly disappeared. What was left he tamped out in the ashtray.

"What do you think they are?" Kentavious nervously asked him, trying to mask the lilting timbre that arose in his voice when he got excited. Years arguing with white people at Bucknell then at Swarthmore had taken snatches of bass out of his voice, especially when he got angry or felt some nervous pull on his spine, that pinch in his stomach that told him a difficult conversation was coming. Hearing his own voice, seeing the gun, he was shocked that he had agreed to come back to John's place to smoke at all. He hadn't smoked since college, he reminded himself; he always wanted to be fully aware and conscious and "substance-free," or whatever, if he was ever accosted by the cops at a protest or, hell, on a routine walk to the store. He thought, like the other twentysomethings fresh from a Fanon re-read and a handful of Omali Yeshitela seminars that the work he was doing documenting protests, taking pictures that could be used to dox abusive cops or white supremacists, was the kind of work that got agents on his tail. Black cars made him flinch. He looked at the gun and thought about Fred Hampton and George Jackson and Assata Shakur walking the streets before things went down, and he slowly slipped out of his puffer, stiffening up a little. With a huskier tone he asked, "Those machines. What do you think they are?"

"Bruh, I'on't know. Like them jawns just appeared out of nowhere." John's words hung in the air. Hearing them felt . . . sweet. Comforting. Kentavious devoured much of his food, then closed the lid and pretended to be full. It dawned on him that were it not for the machine in the sky, he probably wouldn't be there, sitting at a drug dealer's mom's dining room table, about to smoke weed for the first time in three years. Those machines pulled people together in weird ways, the static firing off of them igniting some dormant, tribal part in their brains—at least that was what the 'hood silently theorized.

"Well," Kentavious offered, carefully breaking the silence, "you think the government made them, like some kind of tracking system or something? Supposedly they only been spotted like, down in North Philly and here out West. What you think?"

"Man, I don't be thinking about that shit, man," John laughed. "It ain't making me money so—" he said, and laughed harder.

"That's what's up," Kentavious said, eyeing the weed. They smoked. It was potent, but somehow calming. There was an electricity underneath his skin, Kentavious thought, a power. That same ozone-like sensation the machine carried with it, enhanced by the weed. After three hits, Kentavious nervously looked at his phone, catching a glimpse at John as he did, a glimpse that brought forth the first sliver of a sign of insecurity on John's face. A line, then two, wrinkles appeared on John's forehead, slightly hidden by his Afro's overhang, but still noticeable. John's eyes were raised slightly, the kind of gentle nod that belied curiosity.

"What, you gotta be out?" John asked, his voice lower, huskier, tinged with a hint of sadness.

"Nah, just gonna check my messages," Kentavious said. He clicked through some emails, then settled on Scruff. Again. As the app loaded, John's own phone rang. A tinny trap beat and the rasp of Chief Keef burst through the silence. John picked it up—"Yerp," and after a beat his voice raised, and rose again, until he was shouting into the phone. "Bitch, I told you to give him all the money! Give him the fucking money, Latasha, stop fuckin' playin'." At first the rise in John's voice gave Kentavious a start. As a way to settle the unease and to let John's unwieldy conversation float over him, Kentavious snatching couplets of drama ambiently, he frantically pushed further into Scruff. Another faceless avatar. "If these crackers are gonna invade the hood, they could at least show their face," Kentavious mumbled under his breath with needless hostility perhaps inspired by John's rant. He clicked on the faceless profile again. "Sup?" It said. He checked the distance. <1,500 feet. Again.

"Dumb bitch." John's rant was over. John stared across the table from Kentavious with wider eyes.

"What, nigga?"

John slowly rose, his eyes fixed on a window just beyond Kentavious's form. As he passed, John placed a large mitt of a hand on Kentavious's shoulder and kneaded into the flesh, letting it rest there dangerously long. "Don't worry about that," John assured him, feeling Kentavious tremble underneath his touch. Then, in a voice even lower than he'd already used, John said, "That ain't got nothing to do with us."

In the darkness, Kentavious breathed in the musk of John's breath. His head rested in the valley of John's armpit. His hand rested on the ample mound of John's stomach. The two lay on a mattress on the floor, surrounded by Sega cartridges and Xbox game cases and *SLAM* magazines and pizza boxes and shoeboxes and Jordans and Forces, both men wandering in and out of sleep. John would feel for him under the thin duvet, paw at his crotch with calloused hands, slip his briar-like tongue into Kentavious's mouth; John wouldn't groan, just grunt when Kentavious bit down on his nipples, catching a taste of John's sour, smoky pits as he breathed him in. John stayed close to him, pulling Kentavious's body into his, gruffly turning him over, devouring his backside in sloshy laps until John couldn't really breathe, then, after a beat, Kentavious felt the pang of John's dick at his butt. Melting, he spread and let him inside, the man's large body encasing him, legs and arms like tree trunks, feet like hairy clasps, each pump a strange mélange of gentle ease and exhilarating pain. Kentavious fixed his mouth to say, "I don't usually do this . . ." like some ravenous pick-me, but stopped before the words truly formed and instead burrowed his body deeper into John's crevices and let the man do work.

In John's arms Kentavious let his mind drift. Rolling over behind his eyelids IMAX clear was the time in high school when he came out to a friend at a punk rock show and the boy made an "I'm not that way" statement. Kentavious's friend formed the words like a no-homo armor in sun. Then, to the time his band opened an early Cave In show and he came out in the middle of his band's set, this time to everybody else and broke down, and during the second song he ran off stage and up Lancaster Avenue, tears streaming from his face, his hands tucked into his white-belted skinny jeans, his Converse One-Stars loose and flapping in the spring wind. He kept running until he stumbled and fell into a horse. Riding atop the beast was a man in a long duster, his face mapped with tiny keloids and razor bumps spiked with bristled graying hairs, eyes a sharp amber beaming out from under a well-worn, wide-brimmed suede hat. The horse bounded off as Kentavious sat on the curb watching them trot over the horizon. After a while, the muffled sounds of power chords and untuned drums beat rhythm into the stale air. Bearded white boys in gas station jackets, strange white girls with fucked-up bangs and thrift store A-hemmed skirts seemed to materialize on the block as if beamed in—either oblivious or nervous or just flat-out pointing and sniggering. Even in John's arms, with the hard sonics of John's snoring carving notches into his spine like a buzzsaw, Kentavious thought of being left off the chore wheel at the last queer collective house he lived at, a clumsy, passive-aggressive way to smooth kick him out of the house, the chore wheel no longer adorned with his name as if management had written him off the schedule at Red Robin or some shit. When he shuffled a bit, John's arm twitched and instinctively pulled him back in, sinking Kentavious lower into John's hulking body—John, who five or six hours ago, was barely an idea, would not let go.

The room got a little colder. Wind beat against the window until it rattled, until it felt like it would burst out of the frame. John sprang up, a movement so fast that, to Kentavious, it felt like it was being done by another, all different person. John reached under his mattress and pulled out a Glock. He crept to the window and a flash of light popped just outside of it. Kentavious sat up in bed. The circular machine stood there over the street, cracked with light, spiked through with fibrous pins that moved in and out of its circular body. This machine throbbed, stabbed at the air with razor and spire. It seemed to gnash. It was large, too, the circumference wide enough to swallow U-Haul vans stacked two to a side, two on top of those two. It radiated, pulsed. A loud, wet crack, followed by another. The two men could see other young men and women standing outside firing guns at the machine. The people outside weren't angry though, they were jubilant, riding tiny bikes in a circle around it, hollering, tossing empty forty-ounce bottles and firing at them—a gleeful, ghetto skeet shoot in front of an alien machine.

"Damn, they bussin' at the machines now?" Kentavious asked with a lilt.

"Man, they been doin that. Damn, how long were you locked up?" John pulled his pants on over his naked body. Kentavious sighed as John's genitals disappeared into the cheap denim. A white T-shirt and some black Forces later and John, tucking his gun into his waist, said, "I'm finna go out there, that's Pooky and them. I know Yolonda out there, too."

Kentavious stared in awe at the machine. It was colder still, even for autumn, and though his jacket was plenty thick, it wasn't helping. Up close, the machines looked like they moved, like they weren't just static, hard steel in the sky; they looked organic somehow, like layered, hardened wires and filaments tumbling over each other in a circle. And everybody was shooting at it. Or dancing. Or just sitting in their cars listening to Meek with the door open, smoking. Kentavious remembered the weird, palpable sense of dread and ennui that settled in when the machine had disappeared earlier that night and decided he didn't want that feeling again. He would have to meet with a lawyer tomorrow, try to get his case thrown out of court. He would have to start looking for work again since the vegan donut shop that previously employed him was not sympathetic about his stint in the county jail.

John now stood across the street laughing with two men rocking face tattoos. Kentavious nodded at John who just kept smiling, eyes forward, laughing at whatever 'hood tale the tattooed men regaled him with, then turned away from Kentavious and stared, deeply into the machine, John's face frozen in a half smile. Kentavious walked away.

Black cars followed Kentavious on the walk home. They inched along behind him a few feet at a time for two blocks. Nervously, Kentavious fumbled with his phone and keys in his pocket. Finally, they sped away, but slow enough at least though for Kentavious to see that the men in the car were looking straight ahead. He traced their path up the street; they were heading toward light, toward where the winds licked the atmosphere, toward two large, circular machines that hung like ornaments in the sky.

PART II

He showed up at an anarchist community center at the tail end of a book-packing session for prisoners, right before a women's self-defense workshop. He showed up at a Tomi Adeyemi book signing; he hovered by the door of the relatively small bookstore, tucked behind the new release rack, trying to hide his large frame, but the smell of cardamom and a slowly fading swath of Degree Men's UltraClear gave him away. He showed up in the middle of a presentation on the vulnerability of queer Black bodies in activism at one of the cottage houses on the UPenn campus, the rapt silence in the pitch-black room disrupted by the chimed squeak of a door swinging wide enough for him to slip through and then the din of chairs moving along the steely floor. Kentavious held the PowerPoint clicker in his hand and stopped midsentence, an image of enraged people dressed in black, their clothes bloody, faces covered in masks, tears down their cheeks, shouting at the police in full riot gear. Underneath the image, just clicked into view as John took his seat, the words "Who Protects the Most Vulnerable Among Us?"

Kentavious ran out of the small conference room, down the short hallway, and onto the cobblestone campus street. Slowly ambling up the walkway was John, his hands tucked into his hoodie and head bowed. His Forces, splayed to the sides, barely containing his rubbery feet, lurched up the pavement, kicking at unearthed stones and crunching down on autumn twigs. "John," Kentavious called out. "John, wait up." Kentavious jogged to catch up to him. John turned around, cocked his head back, and affected a sly smile.

The two stood in silence, staring off into the green. Evening was creeping in. The sun was a swinging pendulum above the two, a patch of yellow cream melting behind clouds in the maroon and aubergine atmosphere around them.

"Sup, nigga?" John asked, less inquisitive, more accusing. "What you talking about in there?"

"Oh, the lecture? So that was you in there, I thought I could—" he stopped himself. "Anyway, what's up with me? What's up with you, I haven't seen you since that night."

"Been grindin', man. That product not gonna sell itself, you know what I'm sayin'."

Kentavious kicked at a stubborn rock a couple times more than he should have. The air was thick and unseasonably warm. He could feel his lips move as he uttered what he thought were words, found himself tilting on his toes, leaning in toward John, and stuttering. What would he say to him? They held nothing in common except for the exchange of breath, except for the exchange of sturdy, coarse tongue and sweet saliva, for brown arms that could hold a body. That Kentavious could drown in John's arms, could carve out snatches of minutes between hours to sleep there, finding taut nooks for his own slender frame at John's side, was that enough? In the distance a flash cracked; it was faint, but unnatural light parted sheets of night, somewhere deep in their neighborhood. Both men raised their eyebrows, took air deep into their lungs, and pushed it out in huffs. They looked toward the fading sliver in the distant sky and longed for it—they longed for the machine to cut through the tension of the moment, to feel the wiry round wheel, for the circular obelisk to trace its fibers right there, on that Ivy League campus that Kentavious had access to only because his roommate worked as a counselor at the school's LGBT center. He wanted to feel electric again.

"Yeah," Kentavious sighed, slumping his shoulders, his feet flat on the earth. "I just thought—anyway, you came to my lecture. I guess you saw it on Instagram or—"

"Yeah, something like that." A pause. "Listen, I gotta go—see you back in the 'hood?" Kentavious wanted that question to feel like a suggestion, like an invitation; it felt like an ending. A black car rolled up beside them on the sidewalk and opened its back door, triggering Kentavious's still-frazzled, parole-affected nerves. Too many stories, he thought, of the police murdering activists danced through his mind. Lowering his head, tucking back deep into his hoodie, John slumped into the car. His voice was choked and husky when the man across from him, an imperceptible silhouette, pulled the door closed. Through the window Kentavious heard, "We'll smoke again, akhi."

Outside the subway station, the Nu Moors of Judah had set up a table with pamphlets on the machine. They'd changed their entire ideological course seemingly overnight after the machines appeared. Once they would stand out in Center City with a bullhorn, announcing that the birthplace of mankind was in southern Spain, that the Moors were the original man, that the white man and his queer, gay, AIDS-ridden, hypersexual-Black-woman-stealing, Christian barbarism displaced the true seed of the Black man, of the earth. Loudly. Suddenly, Kentavious noticed, they'd shoehorned the machines into their program. The machines were angels, were the souls of ancestors, were portals taking us back to Nu Afrika, a.k.a. Madrid.

They were easily ignored, but increasingly the rabidity surrounding the machines grew. The police were at a loss to contain it, could only make attempts to stop those who danced, who busted shots, who drove empty grocery carts at and toward the pulsating wheels. When the machines would appear the police would just . . . stand there? They got out of their cars and leaned against the doors, sometimes sitting on the hood, their awful black plastic shoes swinging in the headlights. Sometimes they'd take the bullets out and let children play with their guns, shaking their heads the whole time. Then black cars would pull onto the block, slow creeping, stop in front of the cops and yell at them and it would seem to set them upright, though often they'd go back to their duties of crowd dispersal reluctantly. There would be poetry slams at the mouth of the machines, light dancing off the readers. DJs appeared, entire blocks closed down, and the cool breeze, the cackling light, and the ever-moving wires spun around the machines in a frenzied hoop, looping and looping to the throb of the sound system. The more fanatical of the witnesses would say the machines were dancing.

It was movie night, and Cici's time to host. Kentavious got off the subway and walked the rest of the way to his friend's house. It was a light blue, freshly painted row home with stubbly concrete steps and a wide porch replete with butterflies and moths batting their papery wings by the porch light. He braced himself, knowing that some of Cici's strange, white roommates—particularly the ones that had started a Zumba class/avant garde folk-punk collective—would be milling about. "We take Indian and Indigenous and African folk songs," one of them spoke from stage at a show Kentavious had been dragged to, "and we reshape them to fit our lives here, living in the culturally rich confines of West Philadelphia." They replaced war chants and ablutions and lyrical offerings to the L'wah with stories about missing brunch with their girlfriends and how scared they are at night walking around their own neighborhoods while hanging up missing cat signs on light poles.

He went to knock but saw it was open and since he was late and expected, he pushed the heavy door and walked in. John was on the couch, lying face up and breathing erratically. Cici rushed into the living room with a damp, hot towel and pressed it onto John's forehead. Her roommates were darting about the house, digging through their cupboards for stuff like Echinacea and other roots; one came in carrying a bottle of horse vitamins.

"Kent! This guy says he knows you?"

"John, what the fuck? How do you even—what are you doing here, dude?" Kentavious's voice was a harsh, raspy whisper. He wanted to scream but when he saw the cuts and welts and lacerations on John's face, on his torso beneath the sweat-slicked and bloodied T-shirt, he could only fall to his knees before the couch and stare at him. "What—what happened?"

John rolled over, the towel falling onto the floor. He groaned.

"He doesn't want us to call the police or an ambulance," Cici said. Her beautiful dark-brown face was stone. She was looking forward to watching *Fargo* and she didn't like a lot of 'hood shit and was never approving of Kentavious's dabbling. He looked back at her with equal intensity, then back toward John. In a move that felt strange, he grabbed John's hand and cupped it, then brought it to his lips and kissed it. Kentavious could feel Cici's eyes growing wide, her roommates' eyes, once they stopped looking for natural remedies to help John, growing even wider. Kentavious picked up the towel and put it back on John's forehead and John grimaced.

"Okay, I'm calling an ambulance," Kentavious beamed. Cici's phone was already out, ready to dial.

"NO!" John screamed, tearing upright on the couch, his voice echoing through the cavernous row home, bouncing off the cobbled-together bikes, ricocheting off the mulch basket and up past the second-wave feminist fanzine clippings hung up on the walls in place of art. "No ambulance. No cops." His voice once boomed, now whispered. "I've seen the way the sun pulls at the stars, I understand ley lines now, and I know the integers in the final equation of time and of space. I know how to become tachyon and lightning, faster speed and speed faster. I know the longitudinal Doppler equations, I know fission. Or is it fusion?" His eyes rolled up into his head and he collapsed.

"Jesus!" one of the roommates screamed.

"John! John, you in there?" Kentavious gently slapped John's face, then again harder. "We have to call the police, John!"

"They won't get here in time. The hospital's not far, here, I'll drive you, can you lift him up?" Cici already had her keys out. She slung a small bag around her shoulders and walked up to Kentavious, her hand resting on his shoulder. "He's breathing. Deeply. So he's good. Let's just get him out of here."

Kentavious stared long into John's eyes, a second wrapped in an eternity. Those eyes were a dulled amber, rolling around the pupils. Kentavious glanced toward the backseat of Cici's car; John's arms were extended toward the roof, his mouth agape. He was mouthing hushed, breathless tones, inaudible except a few words: ". . . god . . .

jubilee . . . sanctuary . . . corndog . . . corona . . . eclipse . . . Brexit . . ."
Cici's focus on the road shifted when Kentavious reached back and
tried to calm John, touching the man on his forehead, John writhing, twisting, and recoiling at every touch, his murmuring stunted
and glitchy.

"What are you doing? No, don't touch him," Cici said. "This looks—
fuck, am I even saying this? This looks like machine infection, like
they teach you in—he could have a fever or get all seizure-y or . . ."

"Cici! The road!"

The crash was a loud thud, metal ripping on metal. Cici slammed forward and smacked her head on the steering wheel; a sharp, magnetic
tap that sounded almost as loud as the wreck itself, then snapped
back onto her seat by her seat belt. She was out cold. John slammed
against the back of the front seat, his body large and heavy enough to
uproot the headrest that Kentavious saw flash in front of his vision,
a slow sludgy image of a piece of Cici's car sent flying before him to
wedge into the windshield. Kentavious wasn't wearing his seat belt,
so he followed it. The glass cracked gently when he hit it. Kentavious
crumpled to the floor, hitting his face on the now-opened glove com-
partment. His neck felt strained, his side ached, his vision blurred,
head spun.

He crawled out of the car. Lightning rose around him, it seemed, as
a little of his blood mixed with a little glass. Sharp blue lights danced
in the middle of the street. The passenger in the car they had hit
came running out of her car, screaming. A white woman with poorly
groomed dreadlocks, baggy cargo pants, and a sports bra, berating
him about insurance rates, her poor hybrid.

A loud crack, and then another. Cars were careening into each other
at a dizzying rate. Drivers piled out of the front seats as SUVs and

Honda Accords piled up before the light. Some folks stood dazed, others shouted demonstratively. Kentavious, still hazy, his vision and hearing fuzzy, slowly walked up the street, peering into the smashed cars. Black men lay crumpled up on the back seat, some cradled in blankets with Navajo patterns, others wrapped in John Varvatos suit jackets, some barely clothed at all; they all murmured and mumbled and raised their arms, their eyes turning a sick beige, rolling up into the sockets. They were large men, black-skinned, pouty lips, unkempt hair, and possessed of a bewildering beauty. They were all John.

The street lights popped off. The ground around them hummed, gravel and glass lifted gently off the ground in the pitch blackness. And in a flash, the largest circular machine Kentavious had ever seen materialized in the vast open air, bursting with blue embers, sparking. It moved, weaving its tentacles of living, black metallic organisms around each other, prickly like a crown of thorns, but not stiff—liquefied branches that ebbed, bobbed, and amalgamated into each other. It stood larger than several of the West Philly row houses it loomed over put together. Behind it, several others popped into existence, and with them the force of a chi-like wind pushing trees and debris. All the drivers stood before the spheres: a Jewish counselor from a West Philadelphia high school who hadn't worked since they found asbestos in one of the gymnasium walls in front of his Prius; a single white mom still in her CVS uniform standing in front of her aunt's gray station wagon; an affluent Indian doctor covered in blood; a white trans man whose lab coat was shredded, the arms of his stethoscope bent, slumped over his black Kia; two fat white men in leather bands and bondage chest plates carrying chains emerging out of a Chevette; the white woman with dreads; and Kentavious. What looked like liquid arms traced their bodies and dove into the cars, coated them with their onyx goo, hardened, and turned to ash. In a bright flash, the discs disappeared.

PART III

Kentavious was late. He opened the auditorium door. It swung open heavy, scraped along the floor, and loudly announced his presence. He stood at the back of the room a bit as a man spoke at the podium. The sound of his voice drummed, sounded hollow. Kentavious could only stare at the folding table of picked-through donuts and souring coffee, Lipton tea. He let out a sigh and leaned against the wall. No one turned to look at him though surely they heard him come in. They were all mesmerized by the speaker. Kentavious heard them collectively chuckle.

"But that was his way," the speaker said, sighing through the laughter. "That—that was his way." He bit his fist and waved his hand and walked away from the podium.

A white man in a dull tweed sport jacket took stage. "Thank you, Josue. Give it up for Josue, everyone." There was light, reverential applause. "It's—it's not easy," the white man began. "It's never going to be easy. He came into our life, I think each of us, at a time that we didn't know we needed him. I was—having trouble at home, with the wife and the kids—two daughters, growing fast. I was drinking, staying out late, the guys at the office, they didn't want to talk to me anymore, I was neglecting my work. It was fine, I told myself. The spreadsheets, the trips to Des Moines. It all seemed so . . . alien to me. You know? And he came into my life, just—appeared. Out of nowhere. A bear in a den of lions." The man paused. Someone coughed. Eyes glassed over. "You know, everyone's going to be talking about the giant discs from outer space, everyone is going to tell their grandkids about the—about the alien machines. I swear to you, and this may sound wild, but—if it wasn't for the YouTubes and the TikToks, I'd never be able to tell you what they actually looked like. All I remember . . . is John."

Everyone clapped, first slowly, then uproariously. They all stood, wiping away tears. Kentavious slid a piece of a lemon cake donut in his mouth, the tangy aftertaste of the dessert tray scraps reminding him of ozone. He wanted to clap, too, but instead he kept eating. He just let the applause and the amens thunder around him. Kentavious clenched his jaw and stared into the cavernous void of the auditorium when the white man at the podium caught his eye and waved him frantically toward the stage, desperate for his story, to hear him tell it.

10 COMMANDMENTS OF BLACK PUNK ACCORDING TO MATT DAVIS COMIC

DR. JOANNA DAVIS-MCELLIGATT

"Black punk means liberation, it means doing things for myself, it means family, it means joy, it means healthy rage, it means radical self-acceptance. Black people plus punk rock equals me."

10 Commandments of BLACK PUNK

According to MATT DAVIS

by jo davis-mcelligatt hissler

My brother Matt died in 2003 — he was 26. At the time, he was touring with his band, Ten Grand, and had been featured in the documentary AFROPUNK. Matt has always been the most punk person I've ever known. In his short life, he worked hard to embody the ethos of DIY, of community building, of intentional outsiderism. He was also one of the people who taught me that being Black is not anathema to being punk, that being Black and being punk are the same. "Black people plus punk equals me," Matt said in AFROPUNK. That still rings true for me. These commandments are full of memories, good words, and bits of advice he gave me over the years. I still find it all useful.

1. You can — and when possible should — DO IT YOURSELF.

2. Love your family and your friends zealously.
(Matt, Dan and me in 1985)

①

③: Fight back. Don't let white kids steal your joy.

④: Know who you are at every age. (Matt and me at 14 and 11)

MATTHEW DAVID DAVIS
DEC 16 1976
AUG 10 2003
Beloved Son Friend
FREE IN CHRIST   JOHN 8:31-32

⑤: There is no time, and God is perfect—
So do what you want—what you can—
With your one life. We all die, but we don't end.

②

6: Be generous with your love.

7: Your Blackness is a gift given to you. No one can have it or take it away. Love your Blackness.

③

8. Things fall apart so you have to be flexible. Don't get too comfortable.

9. Stick to your plan — you can create things only by making them. Can't stop, won't stop, don't stop.

10: Keep it moving.

4

BRONTEZ PURNELL

NONFICTION

INTERVIEW BY
JAMES SPOONER
AND CHRIS L.
TERRY

"Creativity all
happens at once.
There are some
breaks you have to
take. It's in
between the breaks
that other ideas
pop up. It all
fucking
flows."

THERE'S A CHAPTER IN BRONTEZ PURNELL'S LATEST BOOK, *100 Boyfriends*, where the narrator hooks up with a stranger in the basement of a half-renovated house, feeling night air on his skin through unfinished windows. It's intimate and detailed, bringing the reader close to the moment, then the narrator's mind wanders and he muses that he's never gotten fucked and appreciated architecture at the same time. It's a spit-take laugh in the middle of a moment that's poetic and filthy.

Since his days making zines in the mid-1990s, Brontez's writing has always threaded humor and desire through its beauty and vulnerability. And this mix of thoughtfulness and spontaneity comes through in the songs he writes as well—for his solo projects and bands, like the Younger Lovers.

If you want to see what it looks like to move into adulthood while adding nuance and complexity to your creativity, look no further than Brontez Purnell. As a creator, he's always growing, moving from zines to award-winning books, from back-up dancer to founder of a dance school. He's constantly creating, working in different mediums, and it was exciting to have the chance to talk to him.

We interviewed Brontez in James's tattoo studio, Monocle Tattoo, on March 20, 2022. The conversation touched on the surprising themes and ideas that were bouncing around our heads while James and I were making this book, so we thought it would be a good thing to put at the end—like a "making of" scene during the credits. And, yes, Brontez left that day with a fresh tattoo.

—Chris

James

Think I need to make this whole thing a little smaller. Because it's like kind of in your hairline a little bit. And we could fit it in there a little.

Brontez

I love that. Okay, now here's the thing.
I wanted it a tiny bit bigger.

James

Bigger? Okay. So. No problem. Let me take it off of you. You want it like 10 percent bigger?

Brontez

That's what my date said.

James

Do you feel like it's a race against time, getting ideas materialized?

Brontez

I used to feel that way. Now, it's like, there's so much out there, they'll get this one. When I went into a [TV] writers' room for the first time, that was a mind flip.

James

Are you very much a collaborator?

Brontez

Yeah, actually, my whole life has been about community-ality and not doing whatever the fuck I feel like because I have to wait on five other people. But it's different in a room with nine different people just spitting, spitting, spitting, spitting, and having to write every day. And at first I felt negatively about it. But then also, I was like, what is this belief that as a person that creates, I must sit in a room and dream upon my most perfect thing? It's also like, No, you're a writer, it's a job. It flipped this other muscle in me. You should be able to do both.

Chris

You need to collaborate and work solo? Or do it under constraints?

Brontez

Well, do the constraints, and also do the soloist kind of thing. I think writers think a little too much of themselves sometimes because it's an isolationist practice.

James

I was just reading your articles for Shotgun Seamstress. So going from that, which is just like the DIY-est zine, to working in Hollywood. What's the trajectory? How did that happen?

Brontez

I've been writing zines since I was thirteen. I've always done that.

James

The zine part is accessible. The three of us, and a lot of people who are reading the book, already know they can make a zine. But how do you write for Hollywood?

Brontez

First of all, I don't think everyone thinks they can make a zine. When I was in my art program at Berkeley, they also let people in the program that had just started making art, and so much of art is people giving themselves the permission to do something. So, if I made a zine at thirteen, it's probably inherent that I was going to write for something, eventually.

Chris

Just kind of keep developing?

James

As a punk kid, it probably took me until my late twenties to re-alize how extraordinary it was that I had a zine, I had a record label, all this stuff that all my punk peers have.

Brontez

There's so many factors that went into why I felt the need to do that.

In the '90s, I think reading snippets of the Bikini Kill zines, and really believing that you had to take culture into your own hands. Plus, I remember my mother wrote a book. She would come home and just write in this tablet. And she wanted to do that. My aunt, I remember reading some of her poems when I was younger. I think that was part of it.

But also, there was this woman in our neighborhood that had written this self-published book, that I've never been able to find. I remember her because she was on *Geraldo* one time with her daugh-ter, because her daughter had sex as a teenager—back when that could get you on TV. And they had a fuckin' square-ass white girl on the panel that was part of some virginity organization. The woman who wrote the book was defending her daughter. She was like, "Well, lucky for you to keep your virginity. I was raped the first time."

There were several radicalizing points.

I was always talking. I was like my mom, I was just a talker. And people would say shit like, "You should be a preacher one day"— really coded language for "You're a faggot, and you know how to talk to people." And that's another thing. They were like, "Well, you know how to talk to white people." Because they were always putting me in these AP classes and stuff like that.

As far as Hollywood, I'll say it like this: We live in a way differ-ent society than when we grew up with broadcast television. And so when I go into the room the first time they're like, "We're competing in a world and there's 196 shows every six months now." So I think being a TV writer at this point is the same as being a weed trimmer.

Chris

Like, it's just a craft and a lot of people are doing it? It's a hard job? Or what do you mean?

Brontez

It will become more common.

James

Okay, look at this. And then just tell me like, does it need to be smaller and by how much?

Brontez

Smaller by maybe 10 percent.

James

Have you ever or do you still feel like a fraud? Like, an artist waiting to get found out?

Brontez

Sigh Good question. Sometimes I feel like I've had more success than the people who inspired me, and that's totally humbling.

James

Do you feel deserving?

Brontez

Oh, yeah, yes, I feel deserving. But of course, I have that artist thing where I'm never truly satisfied. That's definitely more the feeling. I don't question myself anymore, after being in more professional spaces.

The real tragedy I think of art, especially broadcast media, is how many type-A people have type-B jobs like writing and creating, where you're supposed to be sensitive, blah, blah, blah.

Chris

So, it's like someone that you wish would be doing something intuitive is trying to make a formula?

Brontez

Well, yeah. But that's also the problem, because it takes a type-A person to meet deadlines. So it's this whole structural conundrum that happens.

James

Do you ever meet people who are so creative or so smart and maybe they do what you're doing better? And then it kind of makes you feel like, "Man, why am I even doing this?"

Brontez

There's definitely people whose style I covet, or I feel like they do it in a more efficient way. But, keep yourself from comparing, which I think just puts you in a sinkhole.

The only person I'm competing with is myself.

Chris

Tell me more about an artist not being truly satisfied. I was talking to one of my students a few days ago about how something good happens and it just opens up this black hole that I've got to fill with other good things.

Brontez

Yeah. There was a Martha Graham quote, where she says that the artist is always divinely dissatisfied. Which I think is probably also some workaholic shit. But, yeah, you're always perfecting it, or that's the difference between practice as practice and, just, commerce.

The art practice program I went to at UC Berkeley, they give you a studio for two years, and you just make things and like, talk about it. But I think the thing you're trying to walk away with is, your art is this lifetime practice that you have a relationship with. It's always changing and forming and reforming. And it's your relationship to the practice—the journey, not the destination—that you're supposed to be in love with.

So, when I took ballet, and they're just like, "Practice this many times a day, and blah, blah, blah. You'll never have perfect form and that's the beauty."

Chris

How did you start dancing?

Brontez

I fucking was at Laney College, just walking past the dance studio, and they had this Haitian company. And this woman Collette recruited me for her contemporary Haitian company. And so I danced with them for about seven years, and I trained with this other West African company at this place for another set of years. And it was rad. You know, that's how I got into like ATR—African Traditional Religion—and all this stuff. Which is what helped me keep playing rock and roll, actually.

Chris

How so?

Brontez

I inherently have so many problems with rock and roll. I just play it out of tradition, and because I'm the last man in my family to play it, but also in African Traditional Religion the main thing you're supposed to go away with is singing and drumming is how you connect to spirit. And so I was like, Oh, playing rock and roll is my ATR practice. That and, you know, my granduncle and my great-grandfather were blues musicians, so it's just a personal altar.

Chris

A nice surprise about working on this book is hearing the ways that people are getting inspiration from past generations of their family. I came in thinking about punk as forever looking for something new, creating something new, fuck the past. And that's not what we're really hearing.

Brontez

That's also my problem with rock and roll in general. As '90s kids, we were told that we were different or cool because we were playing rock and roll, when it's also like . . . rock and roll is the most American pastime you can think of.

Also, coupled with the fact that it is this fuckin' white supremacist thing. A couple of years ago I was watching Iggy Pop complaining about the fact that an EDM DJ was playing after him. I was like, What the fuck did you and your generation do that you think was so fucking amazing? Because you can play four chords on the guitar, you are inherently more celestial and intellectual than someone playing EDM?

When you think about the fact that electronic music is a scene that contains living people of color, homosexuals. White rock and roll, after they stole it from Black people, has not changed in coming up on one hundred years. Nothing to be proud of. It creates this horrible conundrum, which is why I named my last record *White Boy Music*.

I'm thinking about the fact that my uncle worked at Galaxy Records alongside Creedence Clearwater Revival, this band that cosplayed as a Louisiana band. They're from El Cerrito. And my uncle's at Galaxy Records, writing like two hundred songs, and they never uplifted him. Like the white men from El Cerrito that's pretending to be niggas is who made all that money?

I still feel in that lineage, too, where it's a struggle. Generationally,

I am doing slightly better, but I do also feel like I play this really archaic form of bullshit or whatever.

James

It seems like you're conscious of playing a role to a community or to your fans.

Brontez

Yeah, definitely that. But also, Kathleen Hanna has this new song ["Mirrorball"] and one of her lyrics is just like, "Stay true to your brand. Stay true to your personal brand." And I'm like, Yeah, why not? I've been doing it this long, I might as well. I want to keep making it until I'm personally satisfied, but luckily, I'm never satisfied.

> **Brontez**
> *Okay, listen. You're gonna hate me. I want 10 percent bigger.*
> *Yes, perfect. I love that. Okay.*
> *[sounds of tattooing ensue]*

James

When I was in my twenties, while I was still making *Afro-Punk*, I was dating this girl who had a Haitian dance company. She was obsessed with finding the lineage between African dance and hip-hop dance. One time, she came into my editing room while I was editing a Cipher show [for the *Afro-Punk* documentary], and there's this one clip where two kids in the pit happen to be doing this windmill thing at the same time, but they were so in sync that it looked like that other kind of African dance.

In that moment, people were talking about moshing as being this crazy white boy shit. We started looking for examples [of moshing in other forms of dance], and saw in Go-Go, they have a dance called roughing it off, and it looks just like a mosh pit.

Chris

Or when they lift the couple up in chairs then run in a circle and dance the hora at Jewish weddings.

James

I think that dance eventually has to touch that level of the movement. Our bodies react to beats in only so many ways.

I don't meet very many punks who have a connection to Haitian dance. And it just reminded me that I spent like four years with this woman and we were constantly comparing. She wasn't part of the punk scene, but she would always come to my things or she would, like, look over my shoulder while I'm editing and name some rhythm the drummer's doing.

Brontez

I think that's the biggest connection between the Americans and who colonized who. They got to keep vodun in Haiti because they were colonized by the French, and Catholics, who let them keep their drums and rhythms. I was reading *Black Spartacus*, that book about Toussaint Louverture that just came out from FSG. What I never knew is that in Haiti at the time, there was only forty thousand white people and five hundred thousand slaves. That is why they got to take that shit over.

Compare that to slaves that landed in, say, Virginia. If you were colonized by the English, they took away your drums. They were afraid of you communicating. Plus, there were more white people watching you. But that tradition pops up in Southern Baptist religion. I look back and think, Oh wait, we used to scream our heads off in church and fall out? That came from this ecstatic culture? Of course we would be in a punk band after that, you know?

Also, I went to an HBCU: Alabama A&M, which is where my parents met. I was conceived there. But our tradition of dancing pops up there. Because you can totally relate that Southern band tradition to everything we do. And even though the colonization signifiers are different, the majors pop up.

James
And I'm sorry, can I have you—I need to get you flat on your side. So you need me to—is this chair okay? More flatter or—?

Brontez
This is great actually.

Chris

Something that really touched me reading your novel *100 Boyfriends* was the talk about looking for elders in the gay community when so many members of the older generation had died off. Tell me more about helping younger people find their way in the world.

Brontez

When I was twenty-five, I started dating this guy that was sixty-five. We met at a bar called Daddy's and you know it was a summer love, like kind of crazy, funny. But, of course, I was a young artist who reminded him of himself.

And the problem I think, too, is most gay men are very ageist. This article that came out said we love to memorialize the victims, but a lot of those men didn't die. How do we take care of our older men that didn't die?

And the other thing is, I don't like hanging out with young people because there's also the belief that there's something for me to teach them.

Chris

I feel myself butting up against that, too. When I was younger, my attitude was, "Fuck you, old man. I'm gonna do my thing." Now, I still feel like that sometimes . . . but I'm the old man. And, that can curdle into something bad. It doesn't age well. I'm struggling with that.

Brontez

And also, we are softer than the generation before us. I look at my dad's generation, and it's them coming out of this Southern rural-ness. They came from a farm community where children were literal property. We were the first generation that came out of that in a way different way. So when I talk to people younger than me, my first thing is: Don't do anything I did. Maybe that's also from being in the Bay and all my teachers being like, "There's no such thing as a teacher."

I never want to establish any type of, like, sagely advice, because I feel like my life has been hard and fucked up. And now, you can do the opposite of what I did. Whereas my father's generation, they really had that relation to patriarchal power that they never questioned, much to their detriment. So, when my younger nieces and nephews have contempt for me if I tell them to do something, I really like that because I feel like I didn't have that. And that's why we were the generation that ended up on milk cartons. Because we were taught not to question adults.

Chris

You can think for yourself and rebel, but brush your fucking teeth.

James

I really value the human relationship that I have with my kid. She's a kid, so she's an idiot. She doesn't want to drink water or eat breakfast or lunch. And then she's wondering why she's exhausted at the end of the day. But there's a lot of things that she teaches me as well. And I don't think that a lot of people in our generation have that kind of relationship with their parents.

Chris

A reciprocity?

James

Yeah. I was scared to death of my dad until I was, like, thirteen years old. I used to repeat everything I was going to say to him before

I said it several times, just to make sure that . . . I don't even know what I was expecting him to do, but I just was scared. I definitely don't have that relationship with my kids.

Brontez

My nieces and nephews are generationally so different. I grew up in my grandmother's house with all my cousins, and I remember just walking the road and the oldest amongst us being twelve, whereas my nieces and nephews have never spent more than, like, twenty minutes outside of adult supervision. They even act different.

I think that is why I could be a punk, why I could live in a warehouse with twenty people. I was raised in a nation of kids, this kind of feral childhood that just would not go down these days. We're way more precious of childhood than in the '80s.

James

We were the most unparented generation in history. That was the first generation where women got to work, or where both parents had to go to work and kids raised themselves. Divorce, all that stuff, you know?

We're also a lot more vocal about the dangers out there. My kid knows that my expectation is that if she has a sleepover, she's going to get plastered. So that's why it doesn't happen. It's just erring on the side of caution, because that shit does happen.

It sounds like we all kind of had the same situation where, at a certain point in teenage life, going out for the weekend was all right.

Brontez

My mother was very strict in this way, too. She had me home on graduation night at ten o'clock.

I'm so not protected in other ways, but I was more or less a repressed youth. That's what made my twenties so wild. I just never had that space in my teens. So by the time I was in my twenties in the Bay, spiritually, I was a teenager.

James

Did you move from Alabama to Oakland?

Brontez

No, I lived in Chattanooga for a bit, then I lived in Indiana for a couple months, and then I moved out to California.

James

Was Oakland the first big city where you could just go to a gay bar, or hang out with gay people?

Brontez

Yes. In that sort of manner, yes.

James

I imagine that would be a recipe for, like, let's fucking party.

Brontez

In the space of a year and a half, I was at my mom's house in my room and then I was in Oakland onstage in my underwear dancing in front of a bunch of boys that wanted to give me drugs, and I was like, no wonder . . .

After that Ghost Ship fire, all the warehouse spaces pretty much closed down. Also, people don't really listen to indie rock like they used to. I think it's funny, the person who recorded me's dad moved here with him from Alabama and we were just like, How on earth did we make it from Alabama to California in a van with no license plate, no registration, our entire life in that van, maybe three hundred dollars among us? The gas money alone you couldn't do.

James

I feel like inability to tour is a contributing factor to the fall of rock and roll. It used to be, three hundred dollars would get you gas around the entire country.

Brontez

Also the signifiers being so different. In the '90s, if you were in the parking lot of Kmart, and you saw a boy with blue hair skateboarding, in eight out of ten scenarios, he was supposed to be someone you know. Whereas now, everybody has that. Those signifiers mean nothing. What's that *Penny Arcade* quote I love? "Who are these young Republicans with multiple piercings?"

James

Nirvana broke in September, and so in August of '92, if you saw somebody with a flannel wrapped around their waist, you knew that was a punk rocker, no question. In November of '92, could be anybody who saw the "Smells Like Teen Spirit" video.

Chris

I have this memory from eighth grade, which would have been '93. I was skateboarding and these two white preppy girls showed up at the skate spot and were sitting on the curb, rapping along to "Nuthin' but a 'G' Thang." Rap was outsider music before that.

James

My high school, we were bused into New Town. And Madison was a military town. If I'd went to the school in the next county over with my cousins, I'd probably have a country accent and wouldn't have had access to punk or anything. The first people I rocked out with were these two Pakistani boys whose dad was an engineer. My first band was with another Black girl whose mom was in the military.

Brontez

Yeah, totally. I look back and it's so funny now. I didn't know how lucky I was that I was placed exactly where I was in like the pressure cooker of it. My first punk band being with a Black girl in Alabama, of all the places in the world. How did I land there? I still talk to her all the time.

James

It really does make a difference when you're not the only one, but if you're also not the first one. If you walked into a space and there's already somebody who is doing the thing, right? And so it not only makes you feel less alone, but it also adds a level of normalcy to it.

Brontez

Totally, but also we hated each other at first. I guess she wanted to be the only Black Riot Grrrl in our school.

James

Okay. I think we're done.

Brontez

OMG. Yes. That's how I fucking feel about it.
What were we talking about?

Chris

You write about sex really well. Really nicely. What advice do you have for someone who wants to do it well?

Brontez

First of all, don't. Just don't.

I've always said that I write anti-erotica. When I first started reading, like, gay men's things, the way they wrote about sex I think is necessary for the time because gay sex was so downplayed, but sometimes that writing is like "his perfect ten-inch cock penetrated my fucking voluptuous . . ."

I write about what's human about sex, or the parts that fuck with us, or the real relational parts of sex. I'm writing about sex, but it's certainly not sexy, which shifts the conversation. The people that have hit me up the most about *100 Boyfriends* are forty-year-old white women. They're just like, "Oh, I love this book. I identify with this," so it speaks to this thing that we all feel.

My first book, *Johnny, Would You Love Me If My Dick Were Bigger?* More straight dudes are like, "Man, I love that title" because there's always a societal fear around dick size. But no straight man would ever write a book about that.

It's funny who pops up when you just write about human beings in a human way.

Chris

Yeah, it hit me in the heart.

Brontez

We're poisoned by porn, and the belief that sex is cinematic. I often try to bring it down to scale.

Chris

Do you want to talk about this tattoo?

Brontez

Um, no.

Photograph by Chris L. Terry at Monocle Tattoo

NO WHITES ON THE MIC

ROUNDTABLE

WHAT'S ON YOUR RADAR THAT'S UP
AND COMING IN THE PUNK SCENE?

What's on your radar that's up and coming in the punk scene?

SHAWNA
Sour Spirit in Philly, love, obsessed, amazing! And then there's Mirrored Fatality in the Bay Area, which are some younger folks. They're really amazing.

SCOUT
Vagina Witchcraft. They are a three-piece doom metal hardcore band from Winnipeg. So good! U.N.I.T. from Texas and The Ire from Philly is still one of my favorites.

CHRISTINA
I'm gonna go ahead and plug Punk Black, mainly because they have so much going on as far as these different channels of delivery and touchpoints. I don't know if you've seen their 24-hour radio station on YouTube, but it's like they've really been trying to come up with ways where they could be a continuous platform. I don't see anybody else moving that way.

STEPHANIE

There's a solo artist called No Home, who's based in London. Also Fraulein, who are a Riot Grrrl–inspired band. Oh, and I forgot Nova Twins from London.

MONIKA

I've been listening to a lot of Soul Glo and Proper.

SHANNA

Fuck You Pay Us is probably one of my favorite Black punk bands, definitely Fuck You Pay Us. And Uhuru, I like them a lot too.

THE *BLACK PUNK NOW* RECORD CRATE

ME AND JAMES PICKED SOME OF OUR FAVORITE BLACK PUNK songs from over the years, and asked this book's contributors to do the same. Here's a list, in alphabetical order, covering a wide variety of punk subgenres—I see a propulsive goth song by The Ire sandwiched between Ipecac's mathy '90s emo and metalcore from Jesus Piece. Every song is different, so start with the first band name that grabs your attention and take it from there—you'll be surprised where it leads you.

—Chris

"Get Out," The 1865
"Godzilla 98' Sux!!!," Arcadia Grey
"Back to Before," Baby Got Back Talk
"Right Brigade," Bad Brains
"Take Your God Out of My Peanut Butter," Bad Reaction
"Just Things," Beefeater
"Confident Man," Big Joanie
"Radiant," Black Spirituals
"Birds," Brown Sugar
"My Rules," Buggin
"Shall Be Judged," BURN
"Vulcan Princess," Stanley Clarke
"Circles (Dag With Shawn version)," Dag Nasty
"RNA in Our DNA," Dead Cassettes
"Politicians in My Eyes," Death
"Beware," Death Grips

"Indulge Me," Debby Friday

"Assimilation," Divide and Dissolve

"Breaker," Dragons of Zynth

"Octavia Butler," Dreamcrusher

"New Wage Slavery," End it

"You're No Good," ESG

"Break It Down," Fireburn

"Daddy Drinks Because You Cry," Ricky Fitts

"I Think I've Had It," The Gories

"Velvet Noose," Husbandry

"I'll Be Deemed a Genius," Ipecac

"The Chariot," The Ire

"Adamant," Jesus Piece

"Pope Will Roll," Light Asylum

"Love Smothers Allergy," Long Fin Killie

"Welfare," MAAFA Hardcore

"Protect and Serve," Minority Threat

"Illegals," The Muslims

"We Need Support," Negro Terror

"The Secret Life," New Bloods

"Too Punk Shakur," Obnox

"FK," Pink Siifu

"Strange Glances," Bobby Porter of Thin White Line

"Prison Strike," Provoke

"Future," Pure Hell

"Noise Addiction," Pure Hell

"Don't Shoot," Rebelmatic

"Deathwire," Rough Francis

"The Universe," Solarized

"31," Soul Glo

"Young, Gifted, Black, in Leather," Special Interest

"Sundown," Squid Ink

"Peat Moss," Stout

"Ghost," Swiz

"Fuck You Guyses Team," Ten Grand

"Shout Away," Truth Cult
"Human Farm," Whipping Boy
"Blue Lights," Winter Wolf
"Identity," X-Ray Spex
"Circumstantial Evidence," Yaphet Kotto
"Tight Fade," The Younger Lovers
"Straight from Da Tribe of Tha Moon," Zulu

ACKNOWLEDGMENTS

JAMES SPOONER AND CHRIS L. TERRY WOULD LIKE TO THANK...

Mensah Demary, Cecilia Flores, and the team at Soft Skull Press.

Our agents Kirby Kim and PJ Mark, plus Eloy Bleifuss at Janklow & Nesbit.

CHRIS

Thank you to...

All the Black punks who I met on the *Black Card* book tour. You inspired me to make this.

James Spooner for editing it with me.

All the contributors for their candor, time, and energy. Thanks for letting us hang out.

D. T. Robbins and Chris Stuck for the notes on my short story.

Salpy Talian for taking time to play out different book cover scenarios.

The crew at *Razorcake Magazine* for keeping me current.

My parents for encouraging me to explore music and art, as a participant and observer (Dad, I'm sorry about the time I blew out your stereo speaker with my bass guitar).

My wife, Sharon, for absolutely getting me like no one else ever has, and proving it by playing random '90s post-hardcore in the car on date night.

My kid, Felix, for "giving me a mosh" when I play punk records at home.

JAMES

Thank you to Chris L. Terry for bringing me on board this project. I'm proud of what we've accomplished together.

Much love to my friends in the scene, who answered the call and contributed to this book. I also want to give love to all the artists who shared a review—your support is a testimony to the strength and generosity of our community.

As always, thank you to my partner, Lisa, who challenges me in the best way every day. Thank you to my co-parent, Tiease. Thank you to my kids, Hollis and Issa. I hope you and your generation benefit from this work, and all work that expands limited notions of Blackness.

Lastly, thank you to all the Black and POC punks, past and present, who continue to inspire me every day.

ABOUT THE CONTRIBUTORS

Originally from Brooklyn, life changed for **KASH ABDULMALIK** (he/him) after hearing Minor Threat. Inspired by the hard work ethic of Black Flag and the razor sharpness of Bad Brains, he moved to Los Angeles and started his band, Bad Reaction. The group toured the country while helping a new wave of hardcore emerge in LA. Now a writer and actor, Kash has multiple projects involving Black rock 'n' roll in the works in film and television, including a biopic of "Screamin'" Jay Hawkins.
@hashtagkashtag | @sonofdengar

HANIF ABDURRAQIB (he/him) is a writer from the east side of Columbus, Ohio.
@nifmuhammad

OSA ATOE (she/her) is an artist, teacher, and ceramicist operating Pottery by Osa, producing small-batch handmade ceramics. Currently residing in Sarasota, Florida, Osa previously lived in Portland, Oregon, and New Orleans, where she primarily made Shotgun Seamstress. Osa is also a punk musician who performed in numerous bands including VHS, New Bloods, and Firebrand.
@shotgunseamstresszine

RAEGHAN BUCHANAN is an illustrator, writer, and musician, born in Erie, Pennsylvania. After spending more than a decade drumming and singing in hardcore, post-punk, and power pop bands, she has returned to her first love: comics. Besides doing industry work-for-hire, she has most recently created self-published books *Strange Glances* and the *POCtober Sketchbook*, as well as the new ongoing series *The Secret History of Black Punk* (Silver Sprocket). Buchanan's creative work centers on exploring different areas of Black heritage such as rock 'n' roll musical roots and Black liberation history.
@peppermint_raygun

SCOUT CARTAGENA (she/they) is from Baltimore, Maryland, but currently resides in Philadelphia, Pennsylvania, as a multidisciplinary sculptor and printmaker. The founder of Break Free Fest, Scout is currently spending their time between being an educator and working artist, when not taking multiple photos of her pets and losing the pencil she *just* had in her hand. @scoutcartagenamakes

MARCUS CLAYTON (he/him) is a multigenre Afro-Latino writer from South Gate, California, who holds an MFA in poetry from Cal State Long Beach. He is an executive editor for *Indicia Literary Journal* and plays in Los Angeles punk band tudors. Currently, he pursues a PhD in literature and creative writing at the University of Southern California, studying the intersections between Latinx literature, Black literature, decolonization, and punk rock. His book of hybrid fiction and nonfiction, *¡PÓNK!*, is forthcoming through Nightboat Books, and his critical work can be found in the *Oxford Handbook of Punk Rock*. Instagram: @marcussomethingsomething | Twitter: @marcussomething

HONEYCHILD COLEMAN (she/her) busked in New York City's subways in 1993 and collaborated with illbient and dub reggae DJs. A cofounder and organizer of Sista Grrrl Riots as of 1998, she worked with the Slits, Mad Professor, the Veldt, and Raz Mesinai. Featured in documentaries *Afro-Punk*, *Sounds of Justice*, *Fireflies*, *Getting My Name Up There*, and *Rock Chicks*, she fronts blues-punk's the 1865 and post-punk's Bachslider. Her songs are in the film *Pariah* and the 1865's music in television series *Woke!* and *Everything's Gonna Be All White*. Her story is from her novel in progress, *BLACK GIRL:BLUE HAIR*. @hccoleman | @the1865band

GOLDEN SUNRISE COLLIER (they/he) is a facilitator and multidisciplinary artist with work in the collections of the Getty Museum Research Institute, the Metropolitan Museum of Art, Ontario College of Art and Design, the Library of Congress, and NYU's Tamiment and Wagner Labor Archives. He is a Chicago Printmaker's Guild member and filmmaker

with works shown across the globe including Melbourne Queer Film Festival, OutFest LA, and more. He loves playing viola, writing letters, gardening, cycling, libraries, wheel throwing, keeping bees, and learning/connecting all kinds of new skills in his spare time.
@d.s.press | @blackqueertransrecovery

CAMILLE A. COLLINS (she/her) has an MFA in creative writing from the School of the Art Institute of Chicago. She has been the recipient of the Short Fiction Prize from the South Carolina Arts Commission, and her writing has appeared in *The Twisted Vine*, a literary journal of Western New Mexico University. Her debut novel, *The Exene Chronicles*, was published by Brain Mill Press in 2018. She likes writing about music and has contributed features and reviews to *Afropunk*, *BUST*, and other publications.
Instagram: @camillecollinsauthor | Twitter: @camilleacollins

SHANNA COLLINS (she/her) is a writer, music organizer, and aspiring DJ who has organized with Black and Brown Punk Show, BBIC (Black Brown Indigenous Crew), and A Tribe Called Cunt. She has written for *VIBE* magazine and co-facilitated a hip-hop poetry workshop series with Brown and Proud Press in Chicago. She currently runs a radio station centering music in the Black Global South.
@djpxssycontrolll

DR. JOANNA DAVIS-MCELLIGATT (she/her) is an assistant professor of Black literary and cultural studies at the University of North Texas. She is the coeditor of *Narratives of Marginalized Identities in Higher Education: Inside and Outside the Academy* and *Narrating History, Home, and Dyaspora: Critical Essays on Edwidge Danticat*. She is at work on her first monograph, entitled *Black Aliens: Navigating Narrative Spacetime in Afrodiasporic Speculative Fiction*. She lives in Denton, Texas, with her partner, son, and three cats.
@jcdmce

LAINA DAWES, PHD (she/her), is an ethnomusicologist, a music critic, cultural commentator, and author of *What Are You Doing Here? A Black*

Woman's Life and Liberation in Heavy Metal (Bazillion Points, 2012, 2020). She currently teaches at Columbia University in New York City.

Instagram: @Writingisfighting | Twitter: @Lainad

MARS DIXON (he/they), originating from the Natural State of Arkansas, has been a Brooklyn resident for over a decade. He's played in several punk bands in the Midwest, Bay Area, and New York. His most notable musical project was called Aye Nako, a Black trans and queer punk/indie band whose songs broached subjects such as isolation, anti-Blackness, childhood trauma, and heartbreak. In true Gemini fashion, he spends his energy on a multitude of passions such as a YouTube gaming channel, sewing, ceramics, writing, and a computer donation project for Black and Brown queer and trans people in need.

@mmdizzie

MARTIN DOUGLAS (he/him) is a veteran music journalist whose work has appeared in *Pitchfork*, Bandcamp Daily, *CREEM, MTV News*, respected hip-hop blog *Passion of the Weiss*, and various other publications. Martin has been writing for KEXP since 2018, where he is a features writer and a contributor to *Sound & Vision* and the podcast *Fresh off the Spaceship*, in addition to running the site's Pacific Northwest music column "Throwaway Style." "Confessions of a Black Rock 'n' Roll Critic" is his first published work of fiction.

Instagram: @theedouglasmartini | Twitter: @douglasmartini

BOBBY HACKNEY JR. (he/him) is the lead vocalist for the Vermont punk band Rough Francis.

@bobbyhackneyjr

ASHAKI M. JACKSON, PHD (she/her), is a social psychologist, program evaluator, and poet. Her work has appeared in *CURA: A Literary Magazine of Art and Action, Midnight Breakfast, McSweeney's,* and *Prairie Schooner,* among other journals and anthologies. The author of two chapter-length books—*Surveillance* (Writ Large Press) and *Language Lesson* (Miel)—Jackson is also publisher at *The Offing* magazine of art and literature. She earned her MFA (poetry) from Antioch University Los Angeles and her doctorate (social psychology) from Claremont Graduate University. She lives in Los Angeles.

@ashakijackson

PIERCE JORDAN (he/him) is a dude who lives in Philly and sings for the band Soul Glo. He loves KBBQ, Hawaiian BBQ, and tequila.

@moneynicca | @soulglophl

AYTI KRALI (he/him) is a cartoonist in the Washington, DC, area. Punk and metal music and the art on the albums, T-shirts, and flyers in the late '80s were major influences on his comics. He traveled with punk bands selling merch throughout the United States and Western Europe in the early 1990s. After decades working as a horticulturist, Ayti reconnected with friends from the punk scene and has been feverishly and joyfully collaborating again. His newer printed work can be found at Birdcage Bottom Books and past work on album covers from Lookout!, Catheter/ Assembly, and Old Glory Records.

@aytikrali

CHRISTINA LONG is the founder and global creative director of #Blkgrls-wurld Zine, the *Heavy Girls* podcast, and Heavy Girls Punk Music Fest. She is a serial entrepreneur, printmaker, musician, and technologist with over a decade of experience launching digital products for major brands in New York City. #Blkgrlswurld Zine is where she gets to have fun and play outside the lines of traditional graphic design, photography, and zine-making.

@blkgrlswurld_zine

COURTNEY LONG (she/her) is an African American writer and music en-thusiast based in Chicago. Long is the senior editor of indie publisher #Blkgrlswurld® and co-host of the podcast *Heavy Girls*. #Blkgrlswurld® celebrates womxn of color who participate in heavy music genres like metalcore, hardcore, punk, and black metal. Zines published by #Blkgrlswurld® can be found in libraries at the Metropolitan Museum of

Art and more. The press has also curated live events featuring diverse musicians in Philadelphia and New York City. When not headbang booty-shaking, Long can be found holed up in the nearest chocolate shop. @wonderzoning

FLORA-MORENA FERREIRA LUCINI, bassist for the 1865 and founder/composer/vocalist for MAAFA Hardcore, is a professional performing, recording, and touring artist originally from Brazil by way of Washington, DC. While working as a jazz bassist in her pre-teens, she discovered punk and hardcore. She quickly made a name for herself as a staple in the DC hardcore/punk scene as both a musician and promoter. After attending Berklee College of Music, Flora translated her work in the DC scene to the NYHC and punk community. Currently she resides in New York City, working as a professional musician, educator, and curator. @flora.from.maafa | @maafahardcore

MONIKA ESTRELLA NEGRA (she/her) is a freelance journalist and film director. Her first short film *Flesh* is about a Black femme serial killer navigating the Chicago DIY punk scene. She has also directed two additional shorts, *They Will Know You by Your Fruit* and *Bitten, a Tragedy*. She is the cofounder of Audre's Revenge Film and Black and Brown Punk Show Chicago, co-host of *Bitches on Comics,* and co-editor for Queer Spec's *Decoded Pride* anthology. She resides in Minneapolis. Instagram: @audres.revenge.film | Twitter: @audrerevenge

KYLE OZERO is a multi-instrumentalist and multimedia artist currently based in Chicago. He composes and records music for the band the Breathing Light, an all-Black punk band that he formed in 2008 while he was attending the HBCU Alabama A&M University. His fine art practice ranges from visual art and performance to political action. He explores themes ranging from classism and white supremacist ideology to existential thought. Inspired by the late Calvin Chaos, he works to highlight the continuing thread of Black contributions to punk, rock, and other alternative subcultures. @kyleozero

STEPHANIE PHILLIPS (she/her) is a Midlands-based arts and culture journalist whose work has appeared in *The Independent, Guardian, The Quietus*, and more. She is the author of *Why Solange Matters*, a nonfiction book analyzing the creative journey of Solange Knowles. Stephanie is also the singer and guitarist in the Black feminist punk band Big Joanie and is part of the collective behind Decolonise Fest, a London-based annual festival celebrating people of color in the punk scene.
Instagram: @steffimusics | Twitter: @Stephanopolus

SHAWNA SHAWNTÉ (they/them) is a queer DJ, musician, and multimedia artist based in Tucson, Arizona, and blessed to have lived from 2005 to 2018 in the Bay Area. Bliss and bass are foundations of their eclectic DJ mixes. They appear in the film *TattleTale Heart* and in the *Hanky Code Series*. They were co-director of Bay Area Rock camp from 2014 to 2018. Shawnté, a self-taught multi-instrumentalist, has played in many bands and is a founding organizer of the Multivrs Is Illuminated: Bay Area Black and Brown Punk Fest. They love to curate spaces where collaboration, music, fun, and freakiness are exalted as revolutionary acts.
@143rd_dimension

ALEX SMITH (he/him) is a sci-fi writer (*The Resistance* web series; *Black Vans* comic book), artist, musician (art-punk bands Solarized, Rainbow Crimes), activist (Metropolarity queer sci-fi collective) and cultural/arts critic (*Pitchfork, The Key, Bandcamp, Philly Gay News*). He is a recipient of the Pew Fellowship in the Arts and author of the sci-fi/cyberpunk/superhero/Afrofuturist short story collection *ARKDUST* from Rosarium Publishing.
@alexoteric

MARIAH STOVALL (she/her)'s first novel, *I Love You So Much It's Killing Us Both*, will be published by Soft Skull Press.
@retiredpunk

ABOUT THE EDITORS

JAMES SPOONER is a graphic novelist, filmmaker, and tattoo artist best known for directing the seminal documentary *Afro-Punk* (2003) and cocreating the Afro Punk Festival. His graphic memoir, *The High Desert*, about being Black in small-town California and finding salvation in punk, came out in 2022.

CHRIS L. TERRY is the author of the novels *Black Card* and *Zero Fade*. Born in 1979 to a Black father and white mother, Terry spent his late teens and early twenties touring as the vocalist for different punk bands from Richmond, Virginia. He has a creative writing MFA from Columbia College Chicago, and now lives and teaches in Los Angeles.